MTLE Minnesota Life Science (9-12)

Teacher Certification Exam
By: Sharon Wynne, M.S.

XAMonline, INC.
Boston

Copyright © 2011 XAMonline, Inc.
All rights reserved. No part of the material protected by this copyright notice may be reproduced or utilized in any form or by any means, electronic or mechanical, including photocopying, recording or by any information storage and retrievable system, without written permission from the copyright holder.

To obtain permission(s) to use the material from this work for any purpose including workshops or seminars, please submit a written request to:

XAMonline, Inc.
25 First Street, Suite 106
Cambridge, MA 02141
Toll Free: 1-800-509-4128
Email: info@xamonline.com
Web: www.xamonline.com
Fax: 1-617-583-5552

Library of Congress Cataloging-in-Publication Data

Wynne, Sharon A.
    Minnesota Life Science (9-12) Teacher Certification / Sharon A. Wynne. -1st ed.
    ISBN: 978-1-60787-080-7
    1. Minnesota Life Science (9-12)   2. Study Guides   3. MTLE
    4. Teachers' Certification & Licensure   5. Careers

Disclaimer:
The opinions expressed in this publication are the sole works of XAMonline and were created independently from the National Education Association, Educational Testing Service, or any State Department of Education, National Evaluation Systems or other testing affiliates.

Between the time of publication and printing, state specific standards as well as testing formats and website information may change that is not included in part or in whole within this product. Sample test questions are developed by XAMonline and reflect similar content as on real tests; however, they are not former tests. XAMonline assembles content that aligns with state standards but makes no claims nor guarantees teacher candidates a passing score. Numerical scores are determined by testing companies such as NES or ETS and then are compared with individual state standards. A passing score varies from state to state.

Printed in the United States of America   œ-1

Minnesota Life Science (9-12)
ISBN: 978-1-60787-080-7

TABLE OF CONTENTS

DOMAIN I   **LIFE SCIENCE RESEARCH AND APPLICATIONS**

COMPETENCY 001   **UNDERSTAND THE PRINCIPLES AND PROCESSES OF SCIENTIFIC INQUIRY IN LIFE SCIENCE**

Skill 1.1   Demonstrating knowledge of the principles and procedures for designing and carrying out life science investigations.. 1

Skill 1.2   Recognizing and evaluating methods and criteria for collecting, organizing, analyzing, and presenting scientific data 1

Skill 1.3   Recognizing and evaluating sources of scientific information (e.g., professional journals, Web sites), their characteristics, and their use........ 4

Skill 1.4   Demonstrating familiarity with tools, equipment, and materials commonly used in life science investigations... 4

Skill 1.5   Demonstrating knowledge of practices for ensuring a safe environment in classroom, laboratory, and field settings.. 5

Skill 1.6   Applying knowledge of ethics and safety guidelines to the acquisition, care, handling, and disposal of living organisms and to the collection of scientific specimens and data 7

COMPETENCY 002   **UNDERSTAND APPLICATIONS OF MATHEMATICS AND COMPUTERS IN LIFE SCIENCE**

Skill 2.1   Applying mathematical concepts and representations (e.g., algebra, equations, graphs) to model and solve quantitative problems in life science and to communicate solutions in a logical and organized manner..
.... 9

Skill 2.2   Using statistics (e.g., mean, standard deviation, chi-square, linear regression, correlation) to describe and analyze experimental and theoretical data 10

Skill 2.3   Demonstrating knowledge of applications of computers in life science (e.g., designing models, selecting appropriate software and hardware) ......
.... 11

COMPETENCY 003   UNDERSTAND THE CONTENT AND METHODS FOR DEVELOPING STUDENTS' CONTENT-AREA READING SKILLS TO SUPPORT THEIR READING AND LEARNING IN LIFE SCIENCE

Skill 3.1   Demonstrating knowledge of key components and processes involved in reading (e.g., vocabulary knowledge, including orthographic and morphological knowledge; background knowledge; knowledge of academic discourse, including the syntactic and organizational structures used in print and digital academic texts; print processing abilities, including decoding skills; use of cognitive and metacognitive skills and strategies) ...
.... 12

Skill 3.2   Demonstrating ability to plan instruction and select strategies that support all students' content-area reading (e.g., differentiating instruction to meet the needs of students with varying reading proficiency levels and linguistic backgrounds, identifying and addressing gaps in students' background knowledge, scaffolding reading tasks for students who experience comprehension difficulties) 13

Skill 3.3   Demonstrating knowledge of explicit strategies for facilitating students' comprehension before, during, and after reading content-area texts and for promoting students' use of comprehension strategies........................ 13

Skill 3.4   Demonstrating knowledge of explicit strategies for promoting students' academic language and vocabulary development, including their knowledge of domain-specific vocabulary words 14

Skill 3.5   Demonstrating knowledge of explicit strategies for developing students' critical literacy skills (e.g., encouraging students to question texts, developing students' ability to analyze texts from multiple viewpoints or perspectives) 14

Skill 3.6   Demonstrating ability to plan instruction and select strategies that support students' reading and understanding of life science texts (e.g., helping students to relate what is read to relevant prior knowledge, to follow laboratory activity instructions, and to interpret diagrams and graphs in terms of scientific content or meaning) 15

DOMAIN II   **MOLECULAR AND CELLULAR LIFE PROCESSES**

COMPETENCY 004   **UNDERSTAND CELLULAR STRUCTURES AND PROCESSES**

Skill 4.1   Recognizing organelles and other cellular structures, their characteristics and functions, and the interactions between organelles and other cellular structures 17

Skill 4.2   Demonstrating knowledge of methods of measurement used to describe cellular structures and physiological processes 20

Skill 4.3   Analyzing how cells respond to changes in their environment to maintain homeostasis (e.g., active transport, exocytosis) 21

Skill 4.4   Demonstrating knowledge of the cellular processes of a given plant or animal cell (e.g., guard cell, muscle cell, phagocyte) 22

COMPETENCY 005   **UNDERSTAND PHOTOSYNTHESIS AND CELLULAR RESPIRATION**

Skill 5.1   Analyzing the structure of chloroplasts and how structure and function are related 23

Skill 5.2   Demonstrating knowledge of the processes involved in the transformation of solar energy into cellular energy, including biochemical pathways (e.g., Calvin cycle) and electron transport 23

Skill 5.3   Analyzing the structure of mitochondria and how structure and function are related 26

Skill 5.4   Demonstrating knowledge of the processes involved in the release of energy stored in food molecules during cellular respiration, including biochemical pathways (e.g., glycolysis, Krebs cycle) and ATP synthesis 27

Skill 5.5   Applying knowledge of structure-function relationships and the relationships between organelles and the cellular environment to **predict** the effect of a given physical or chemical change (e.g., light intensity, pH) on photosynthesis or cellular respiration 30

COMPETENCY 006   **UNDERSTAND THE STRUCTURE AND FUNCTION OF PROTEINS AND THE PROCESS OF PROTEIN SYNTHESIS**

Skill 6.1   Identifying the basic chemical composition and structure of proteins....... 31

Skill 6.2   Demonstrating knowledge of the processes of transcription and translation, including the roles of DNA and RNA 32

Skill 6.3   Predicting the amino acid sequence of a protein from a given codon sequence 32

Skill 6.4   Recognizing the functions of proteins, including enzymes, in living organisms and factors that affect protein function 33

DOMAIN III   **MOLECULAR REPRODUCTION AND HEREDITY**

COMPETENCY 007 UNDERSTAND THE PROCESSES OF MITOSIS AND MEIOSIS

Skill 7.1   Recognizing stages of the cell cycle and factors that affect the division and growth of cells... 35

Skill 7.2   Recognizing the characteristics and behavior of chromosomes in eukaryotic cells 36

Skill 7.3   Demonstrating knowledge of changes in the visibility, arrangement, and number of chromosomes in the various stages of mitosis and meiosis ... 37

Skill 7.4   Analyzing how meiosis and fertilization contribute to genetic variability... 37

Skill 7.5   Applying knowledge of the characteristics of chromosomes and the laws of segregation and independent assortment to explain how sex is determined in humans 39

COMPETENCY 008   **UNDERSTAND THE CONCEPTS AND PRINCIPLES OF HEREDITY**

Skill 8.1   Demonstrating knowledge of how traits are inherited and expressed...... 40

Skill 8.2   Recognizing evidence that a particular characteristic is inherited........... 43

Skill 8.3   Demonstrating knowledge of the application of statistical analyses for describing the results from a given plant or animal breeding experiment 43

Skill 8.4   Applying knowledge of the rules of probability and heredity (e.g., law of independent assortment) to predict the genotypic and phenotypic outcomes of offspring resulting from crosses of parents with given traits, including dominant-recessive, incomplete and co-dominant, polygenic, and sex-linked traits... 44

COMPETENCY 009   **UNDERSTAND GENETIC MUTATIONS AND FACTORS THAT AFFECT THE EXPRESSION OF GENES**

Skill 9.1   Recognizing the relationships between DNA, genes, and chromosomes 45

Skill 9.2   Recognizing different types of mutations (e.g., substitution, deletion) and their effects 47

Skill 9.3   Demonstrating knowledge of how mutations occur and factors that can cause genetic mutations 48

Skill 9.4   Demonstrating knowledge of the control of gene expression in cells 48

Skill 9.5   Analyzing the effects of environmental changes on the expression of genetic traits 48

COMPETENCY 010   **UNDERSTAND THE PROCESSES AND APPLICATIONS OF GENETIC TECHNOLOGY**

Skill 10.1   Recognizing the principles and processes of producing recombinant DNA 49

Skill 10.2   Demonstrating knowledge of applications of genetic technology in the treatment of human diseases 49

Skill 10.3   Demonstrating knowledge of applications of genetic technology in the development of agricultural products 50

DOMAIN IV   **STRUCTURAL AND FUNCTIONAL RELATIONSHIPS**

COMPETENCY 011   **UNDERSTAND THE CHARACTERISTICS AND PROCESSES OF LIFE AND STRUCTURES OF COMMON ORGANISMS**

Skill 11.1   Recognizing characteristics that distinguish living organisms from nonliving things and methods and evidence for determining the presence of life 51

Skill 11.2   Demonstrating knowledge of structures of representative organisms from major taxonomic groups 51

Skill 11.3   Analyzing structural and functional relationships involved in basic life processes (e.g., obtaining nutrients and energy, maintaining homeostasis, reproducing, growing) carried out by organisms from major taxonomic groups 52

COMPETENCY 012   **UNDERSTAND THE STRUCTURES AND FUNCTIONS OF SYSTEMS IN PLANTS AND ANIMALS**

Skill 12.1   Demonstrating knowledge of the relationship between structure and function in the major systems in plants 54

Skill 12.2   Demonstrating knowledge of the relationship between structure and function in the major systems in animals 55

Skill 12.3   Predicting the system function of a given structure based on its characteristics and components 65

COMPETENCY 013   **UNDERSTAND THE HUMAN IMMUNE SYSTEM, HUMAN DISEASES, AND PRINCIPLES OF DISEASE PREVENTION**

Skill 13.1   Recognizing components of the human immune system and their functions 67

Skill 13.2   Demonstrating knowledge of immune system responses that take place in cells, tissues, organs, and organ systems throughout the progression of a given viral, bacterial, fungal, or parasitic disease 68

Skill 13.3   Recognizing causes and characteristics of common human diseases (e.g., influenza, malaria, cancer), including risk factors 68

Skill 13.4   Applying knowledge of methods for preventing or treating common human diseases.. 69

DOMAIN V   **DIVERSITY AND BIOLOGICAL EVOLUTION**

COMPETENCY 014   **UNDERSTAND THE DEVELOPMENT OF ADAPTATIONS IN RESPONSE TO ENVIRONMENTAL STRESSES**

Skill 14.1   Recognizing the relationship between conditions in an organism's environment and the development of adaptations 71

Skill 14.2   Demonstrating knowledge of the range of physical, behavioral, and biochemical adaptations that can occur in response to environmental stresses 71

Skill 14.3   Applying knowledge of biological principles to explain how a specific adaptation of a given species may have developed 73

COMPETENCY 015   **UNDERSTAND THE SIGNIFICANCE OF GENETIC VARIATION WITHIN A POPULATION AND FACTORS THAT INFLUENCE THE RANGE OF PHENOTYPES IN A POPULATION OF A SPECIES**

Skill 15.1   Recognizing sources of genetic variation within a population and ways of representing (e.g., diagrams, statistical relationships) the range of phenotypes in a population in a given environment 74

Skill 15.2   Demonstrating knowledge of factors that can change the frequency of alleles and genotypes in a population (e.g., nonrandom mating, genetic drift, natural selection)... 74

Skill 15.3   Applying the principles of mutation, recombination, and natural selection to predict changes in the range of phenotypes in a species when a change occurs in the environment... 76

Skill 15.4   Demonstrating knowledge of how changes in the range of phenotypes within populations relate to evolution 76

COMPETENCY 016   **UNDERSTAND EVIDENCE OF EVOLUTIONARY RELATIONSHIPS BETWEEN SPECIES**

Skill 16.1   Demonstrating knowledge of significant features of the fossil record 77

Skill 16.2   Applying knowledge of biological principles to explain why some species are found in the fossil record relatively unchanged, while some species have changed and others have gone extinct 77

Skill 16.3   Applying knowledge of the evolutionary tree to explain and predict the morphological and genetic variations between two or more species 78

Skill 16.4   Analyzing fossil, morphological, genetic, and biochemical evidence and their use in determining evolutionary relationships between species....... 78

DOMAIN VI   **INTERDEPENDENCE AND BEHAVIOR OF ORGANISMS**

COMPETENCY 017   **UNDERSTAND RELATIONSHIPS AMONG ORGANISMS AND BETWEEN ORGANISMS AND THEIR ENVIRONMENT**

Skill 17.1   Demonstrating knowledge of the concepts of niche and habitat and of the basic requirements (e.g., nutrients, water, space) of organisms in their environment.. 79

Skill 17.2   Demonstrating knowledge of the interrelationships and interdependence of organisms in a community (e.g., competition, mutualism, parasitism) 80

Skill 17.3   Demonstrating knowledge of methods for investigating and describing the relationships within and between species in an ecosystem and between organisms and their environment... 81

COMPETENCY 018   UNDERSTAND POPULATION DYNAMICS AND SPECIES DIVERSITY

Skill 18.1   Identifying factors that affect the growth rate and size of a population (e.g., carrying capacity, birthrate, migration)..................................... 82

Skill 18.2   Applying knowledge of population dynamics and inter- and intraspecific relationships to explain or predict changes in population sizes of organisms for given changes in an ecosystem 83

Skill 18.3   Demonstrating knowledge of biotic and abiotic factors that influence the diversity of species in an ecosystem and of processes that lead to changes in species composition and diversity over time (e.g., succession). 84

Skill 18.4   Analyzing differences in population size and species diversity between various habitats, ecosystems, or biomes 85

COMPETENCY 019   UNDERSTAND THE CYCLING OF MATTER AND THE FLOW OF ENERGY

Skill 19.1   Demonstrating knowledge of the cycling of a given substance (e.g., carbon, nitrogen, phosphorus) through the living and nonliving components of the biosphere.. 87

Skill 19.2   Analyzing the flow of energy both within a living system and between the system and the biosphere... 88

Skill 19.3   Identifying the roles of various organisms (e.g., producers, decomposers) in the cycling of nutrients and flow of energy 89

COMPETENCY 020   UNDERSTAND THE BEHAVIOR OF ORGANISMS

Skill 20.1   Demonstrating knowledge of behaviors by which organisms respond to environmental changes or interact with organisms of their own and other species... 90

Skill 20.2   Explaining or predicting the behavioral responses of an animal to a given set of interactions or environmental changes....................................... 90

Skill 20.3   Analyzing behavioral responses of a given organism in terms of natural selection.. 90

Skill 20.4   Demonstrating knowledge of methods for observing, measuring, and describing the physical behavior of animals... 90

Sample Test... 92

Answer Key 114

Rigor Table 115

Rationales 116

Section 1 About XAMonline

XAMonline – A Specialty Teacher Certification Company

Created in 1996, XAMonline was the first company to publish study guides for state-specific teacher certification examinations. Founder Sharon Wynne found it frustrating that materials were not available for teacher certification preparation and decided to create the first single, state-specific guide. XAMonline has grown into a company of over 1800 contributors and writers and offers over 300 titles for the entire PRAXIS series and every state examination. No matter what state you plan on teaching in, XAMonline has a unique teacher certification study guide just for you.

XAMonline – Value and Innovation

We are committed to providing value and innovation. Our print-on-demand technology allows us to be the first in the market to reflect changes in test standards and user feedback as they occur. Our guides are written by experienced teachers who are experts in their fields. And, our content reflects the highest standards of quality. Comprehensive practice tests with varied levels of rigor means that your study experience will closely match the actual in-test experience.

To date, XAMonline has helped nearly 600,000 teachers pass their certification or licensing exams. Our commitment to preparation exceeds simply providing the proper material for study - it extends to helping teachers **gain mastery** of the subject matter, giving them the **tools** to become the most effective classroom leaders possible, and ushering today's students toward a **successful future**.

Section 2 About this Study Guide

Purpose of this Guide
Is there a little voice inside of you saying, "Am I ready?" Our goal is to replace that little voice and remove all doubt with a new voice that says, "I AM READY. **Bring it on**!" by offering the highest quality of teacher certification study guides.

Organization of Content
You will see that while every test may start with overlapping general topics, each are very unique in the skills they wish to test. Only XAMonline presents custom content that analyzes deeper than a title, a subarea, or an objective. Only XAMonline presents content and sample test assessments along with **focus statements**, the deepest-level rationale and interpretation of the skills that are unique to the exam.

Title and field number of test
→Each exam has its own name and number. XAMonline's guides are written to give you the content you need to know for the specific exam you are taking. You can be confident when you buy our guide that it contains the information you need to study for the specific test you are taking.

Subareas
→These are the major content categories found on the exam. XAMonline's guides are written to cover all of the subareas found in the test frameworks developed for the exam.

Objectives
→These are standards that are unique to the exam and represent the main subcategories of the subareas/content categories. XAMonline's guides are written to address every specific objective required to pass the exam.

Focus statements
→These are examples and interpretations of the objectives. You find them in parenthesis directly following the objective. They provide detailed examples of the range, type, and level of content that appear on the test questions. **Only XAMonline's guides drill down to this level.**

How do We Compare with Our Competitors?
XAMonline – drills down to the focus statement level
CliffsNotes and REA – organized at the objective level
Kaplan – provides only links to content
MoMedia – content not specific to the test

Each subarea is divided into manageable sections that cover the specific skill areas. Explanations are easy-to-understand and thorough. You'll find that every test answer contains a rejoinder so if you need a refresher or further review after taking the test, you'll know exactly to which section you must return.

How to Use this Book

Our informal polls show that most people begin studying up to 8 weeks prior to the test date, so start early. Then ask yourself some questions: How much do you really know? Are you coming to the test straight from your teacher-education program or are you having to review subjects you haven't considered in 10 years? Either way, take a **diagnostic or assessment test** first. Also, spend time on sample tests so that you become accustomed to the way the actual test will appear.

This guide comes with an online diagnostic test of 30 questions found online at www.XAMonline.com. It is a little boot camp to get you up for the task and reveal things about your compendium of knowledge in general. Although this guide is structured to follow the order of the test, you are not required to study in that order. By finding a time-management and study plan that fits your life you will be more effective. The results of your diagnostic or self-assessment test can be a guide for how to manage your time and point you towards an area that needs more attention.

After taking the diagnostic exam, fill out the **Personalized Study Plan** page at the beginning of each chapter. Review the competencies and skills covered in that chapter and check the boxes that apply to your study needs. If there are sections you already know you can skip, check the "skip it" box. Taking this step will give you a study plan for each chapter.

Week	Activity
8 weeks prior to test	Take a diagnostic test found at www.XAMonline.com
7 weeks prior to test	Build your Personalized Study Plan for each chapter. Check the "skip it" box for sections you feel you are already strong in.
6-3 weeks prior to test	For each of these 4 weeks, choose a content area to study. You don't have to go in the order of the book. It may be that you start with the content that needs the most review. Alternately, you may want to ease yourself into plan by starting with the most familiar material.
2 weeks prior to test	Take the sample test, score it, and create a review plan for the final week before the test.
1 week prior to test	Following your plan (which will likely be aligned with the areas that need the most review) go back and study the sections that align with the questions you may have gotten wrong. Then go back and study the sections related to the questions you answered correctly. If need be, create flashcards and drill yourself on any area that you makes you anxious.

Section 3 About the Minnesota Life Science (9-12) Exam

What is the Minnesota Life Science (9-12) Exam?
The Minnesota Life Science (9-12) exam is meant to assess mastery of the content knowledge required to teach high school life science in Minnesota public schools.

Often **your own state's requirements** determine whether or not you should take any particular test. The most reliable source of information regarding this is your state's Department of Education. This resource should have a complete list of testing centers and dates. Test dates vary by subject area and not all test dates necessarily include your particular test, so be sure to check carefully.

If you are in a teacher-education program, check with the Education Department or the Certification Officer for specific information for testing and testing timelines. The Certification Office should have most of the information you need.

If you choose an alternative route to certification you can either rely on our website at www.XAMonline.com or on the resources provided by an alternative certification program. Many states now have specific agencies devoted to alternative certification and there are some national organizations as well, for example:
National Association for Alternative Certification
http://www.alt-teachercert.org/index.asp

Interpreting Test Results
Contrary to what you may have heard, the results of the Minnesota Life Science (9-12) test are not based on time. More accurately, your score will be based on the raw number of points you earn in each section, the proportion of that section to the entire subtest, and the scaling of the raw score. Raw scores are converted to a scale of 100 to 300. It is likely to your benefit to complete as many questions in the time allotted, but it will not necessarily work to your advantage if you hurry through the test.

Scores are available by email if you request this when you register. Score reports are available 21days after the testing window and posted to your account for 45 days as PDFs. Scores will also be sent to your chosen institution(s).

What's on the Test?
The Minnesota Life Science (9-12) exam is a computer-based test and consists of two subtests, each lasting one hour. You can take one or both subtests at one testing appointment. A scientific calculator is provided with your test. The breakdown of the questions is as follows:

Category	Approximate Number of Questions	Approximate Percentage of the test
SUBTEST 1	50	
I: Life Science Research and		30%

Applications		
II: Molecular and Cellular Life Processes		30%
III: Molecular Reproduction and Heredity		40%
SUBTEST 2	50	
I: Structural and Functional Relationships		30%
II: Diversity and Biological Evolution		30%
III: Interdependence and Behavior of Organisms		40%

Question Types

You're probably thinking, enough already, I want to study! Indulge us a little longer while we explain that there is actually more than one type of multiple-choice question. You can thank us later after you realize how well prepared you are for your exam.

1. **Complete the Statement.** The name says it all. In this question type you'll be asked to choose the correct completion of a given statement. For example: The Dolch Basic Sight Words consist of a relatively short list of words that children should be able to:
   a. Sound out
   b. Know the meaning of
   c. Recognize on sight
   d. Use in a sentence
   The correct answer is C. In order to check your answer, test out the statement by adding the choices to the end of it.

2. **Which of the Following.** One way to test your answer choice for this type of question is to replace the phrase "which of the following" with your selection. Use this example: Which of the following words is one of the twelve most frequently used in children's reading texts:
   a. There
   b. This
   c. The
   d. An
   Don't look! Test your answer. _____ is one of the twelve most frequently used in children's reading texts. Did you guess C? Then you guessed correctly.

3. **Roman Numeral Choices.** This question type is used when there is more than one possible correct answer. For example: Which of the following two arguments accurately supports the use of cooperative learning as an effective method of instruction?
   I. Cooperative learning groups facilitate healthy competition between individuals in the group.

II. Cooperative learning groups allow academic achievers to carry or cover for academic underachievers.

III. Cooperative learning groups make each student in the group accountable for the success of the group.

IV. Cooperative learning groups make it possible for students to reward other group members for achieving.

    A. I and II
    B. II and III
    C. I and III
    D. III and IV

Notice that the question states there are **two** possible answers. It's best to read all the possibilities first before looking at the answer choices. In this case, the correct answer is D.

4. **Negative Questions.** This type of question contains words such as "not," "least," and "except." Each correct answer will be the statement that does **not** fit the situation described in the question. Such as: Multicultural education is **not**

    a. An idea or concept
    b. A "tack-on" to the school curriculum
    c. An educational reform movement
    d. A process

Think to yourself that the statement could be anything but the correct answer. This question form is more open to interpretation than other types, so read carefully and don't forget that you're answering a negative statement.

5. **Questions That Include Graphs, Tables, or Reading Passages.** As ever, read the question carefully. It likely asks for a very specific answer and not broad interpretation of the visual. Here is a simple (though not statistically accurate) example of a graph question: In the following graph in how many years did more men take the NYSTCE exam than women?

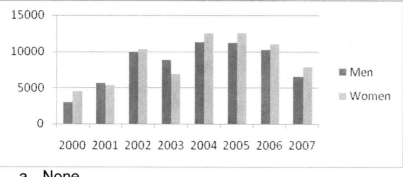

    a. None
    b. One
    c. Two
    d. Three

It may help you to simply circle the two years that answer the question. Make sure you've read the question thoroughly and once you've made your determination, double check your work. The correct answer is C.

Section 4 Helpful Hints

Study Tips

1. **You are what you eat.** Certain foods aid the learning process by releasing natural memory enhancers called CCKs (cholecystokinin) composed of tryptophan, choline, and phenylalanine. All of these chemicals enhance the neurotransmitters associated with memory and certain foods release memory enhancing chemicals. A light meal or snacks from the following foods fall into this category:
   - Milk
   - Nuts and seeds
   - Rice
   - Oats
   - Eggs
   - Turkey
   - Fish

   The better the connections, the more you comprehend!

2. **See the forest for the trees.** In other words, get the concept before you look at the details. One way to do this is to take notes as you read, paraphrasing or summarizing in your own words. Putting the concept in terms that are comfortable and familiar may increase retention.

3. **Question authority.** Ask why, why, why. Pull apart written material paragraph by paragraph and don't forget the captions under the illustrations. For example, if a heading reads *Stream Erosion* put it in the form of a question (why do streams erode? Or what is stream erosion?), and then find the answer within the material. If you train your mind to think in this manner you will learn more and prepare yourself for answering test questions.

4. **Play mind games**. Using your brain for reading or puzzles keeps it flexible. Even with a limited amount of time your brain can take in data (much like a computer) and store it for later use. In ten minutes you can: read two paragraphs (at least), quiz yourself with flash cards, or review notes. Even if you don't fully understand something on the first pass, your mind stores it for recall, which is why frequent reading or review increases chances of retention and comprehension.

5. **The pen is mightier than the sword.** Learn to take great notes. A by-product of our modern culture is that we have grown accustomed to getting our information in short doses. We've subconsciously trained ourselves to assimilate information into neat little packages. Messy notes fragment the flow of information. Your notes can be much clearer with proper formatting. *The Cornell Method* is one such format. This method was popularized in *How to Study in College,* Ninth Edition, by Walter Pauk. You can benefit from the method without purchasing an additional book by simply looking the method up online. Below is a sample of how *The Cornell Method* can be adapted for use with this guide.

← 2 ½" →	6"
Cue Column	**Note Taking Column**
	1. **Record:** During your reading, use the note-taking column to record important points.
	2. **Questions:** As soon as you finish a section, formulate questions based on the notes in the right-hand column. Writing questions helps to clarify meanings, reveal relationships, establish community, and strengthen memory. Also, the writing of questions sets the state for exam study later.
	3. **Recite:** Cover the note-taking column with a sheet of paper. Then, looking at the questions or cue-words in the question and cue column only, say aloud, in your own words, the answers to the questions, facts, or ideas indicated by the cue words.
	4. **Reflect:** Reflect on the material by asking yourself questions.
	5. **Review:** Spend at least ten minutes every week reviewing all your previous notes. Doing so helps you retain ideas and topics for the exam.
↑ 2" ↓	**Summary** After reading, use this space to summarize the notes from each page.

*Adapted from *How to Study in College,* Ninth Edition, by Walter Pauk, ©2008 Wadsworth

6. **Place yourself in exile and set the mood.** Set aside a particular place and time to study that best suits your personal needs and biorhythms. If you're a night person, burn the midnight oil. If you're a morning person set yourself up with some coffee and get to it. Make your study time and place as free from distraction as possible and surround yourself with what you need, be it silence or music. Studies have shown that music can aid in concentration, absorption, and retrieval of information. Not all music, though. Classical music is said to work best.

7. **Get pointed in the right direction.** Use arrows to point to important passages or pieces of information. It's easier to read than a page full of yellow highlights. Highlighting can be used sparingly, but add an arrow to the margin to call attention to it.

8. **Check your budget.** You should at least review all the content material before your test, but allocate the most amount of time to the areas that need the most refreshing. It sounds obvious, but it's easy to forget. You can use the study rubric above to balance your study budget.

The proctor will write the start time where it can be seen and then, later, provide the time remaining, typically 15 minutes before the end of the test.

Testing Tips

1. **Get smart, play dumb.** Sometimes a question is just a question. No one is out to trick you, so don't assume that the test writer is looking for something other than what was asked. Stick to the question as written and don't overanalyze.

2. **Do a double take.** Read test questions and answer choices at least twice because it's easy to miss something, to transpose a word or some letters. If you have no idea what the correct answer is, skip it and come back later if there's time. If you're still clueless, it's okay to guess. Remember, you're scored on the number of questions you answer correctly and you're not penalized for wrong answers. The worst case scenario is that you miss a point from a good guess.

3. **Turn it on its ear.** The syntax of a question can often provide a clue, so make things interesting and turn the question into a statement to see if it changes the meaning or relates better (or worse) to the answer choices.

4. **Get out your magnifying glass.** Look for hidden clues in the questions because it's difficult to write a multiple-choice question without giving away part of the answer in the options presented. In most questions you can readily eliminate one or two potential answers, increasing your chances of answering correctly to 50/50, which will help out if you've skipped a question and gone back to it (see tip #2).

5. **Call it intuition.** Often your first instinct is correct. If you've been studying the content you've likely absorbed something and have subconsciously retained the knowledge. On questions you're not sure about trust your instincts because a first impression is usually correct.

6. **Graffiti.** Sometimes it's a good idea to mark your answers directly on the test booklet and go back to fill in the optical scan sheet later. You don't get extra points for perfectly blackened ovals. If you choose to manage your test this way, be sure not to mismark your answers when you transcribe to the scan sheet.

7. **Become a clock-watcher.** You have a set amount of time to answer the questions. Don't get bogged down laboring over a question you're not sure about when there are ten others you could answer more readily. If you choose to follow the advice of tip #6, be sure you leave time near the end to go back and fill in the scan sheet.

Do the Drill

No matter how prepared you feel it's sometimes a good idea to apply Murphy's Law. So the following tips might seem silly, mundane, or obvious, but we're including them anyway.

1. **Remember, you are what you eat, so bring a snack.** Choose from the list of energizing foods that appear earlier in the introduction.

2. **You're not too sexy for your test.** Wear comfortable clothes. You'll be distracted if your belt is too tight, or if you're too cold or too hot.

3. **Lie to yourself.** Even if you think you're a prompt person, pretend you're not and leave plenty of time to get to the testing center. Map it out ahead of time and do a dry run if you have to. There's no need to add road rage to your list of anxieties.

4. **Bring sharp, number 2 pencils.** It may seem impossible to forget this need from your school days, but you might. And make sure the erasers are intact, too.

5. **No ticket, no test.** Bring your admission ticket as well as **two** forms of identification, including one with a picture and signature. You will not be admitted to the test without these things.

6. **You can't take it with you.** Leave any study aids, dictionaries, notebooks, computers and the like at home. Certain tests **do** allow a scientific or four-function calculator, so check ahead of time if your test does.

7. **Prepare for the desert.** Any time spent on a bathroom break **cannot** be made up later, so use your judgment on the amount you eat or drink.

8. **Quiet, Please!** Keeping your own time is a good idea, but not with a timepiece that has a loud ticker. If you use a watch, take it off and place it nearby but not so that it distracts you. And **silence your cell phone.**

To the best of our ability, we have compiled the content you need to know in this book and in the accompanying online resources. The rest is up to you. You can use the study and testing tips or you can follow your own methods. Either way, you can be confident that there aren't any missing pieces of information and there shouldn't be any surprises in the content on the test.

If you have questions about test fees, registration, electronic testing, or other content verification issues please visit www.mtle.nesinc.com.

Good luck!
Sharon Wynne
Founder, XAMonline

DOMAIN I   LIFE SCIENCE RESEARCH AND APPLICATIONS

COMPETENCY 001   UNDERSTAND THE PRINCIPLES AND PROCESSES OF SCIENTIFIC INQUIRY IN LIFE SCIENCE

Skill 1.1   **Demonstrating knowledge of the principles and procedures for designing and carrying out life science investigations**

Scientific research serves two purposes:

1. To investigate and acquire knowledge that is theoretical
2. To perform research that is of practical value

Science has the unique ability to serve humanity. Scientific research results from inquiry. An inquiring mind is thirsty, trying to find answers. An inquisitive person asks questions and wants to find answers. The two most important questions—why and how—are the starting points of all scientific inquiry.

Scientific research uses the scientific method to answer questions. Researchers follow the scientific method, which consists of a series of steps designed to solve a problem. The aim of the scientific method is to eliminate any bias or prejudice that the scientist or researcher might bring to the inquiry. If the researcher follows all the steps of the scientific method as outlined, the research is as free from bias as possible.

The scientific method consists of the following steps:

1. Stating the problem clearly and precisely
2. Gathering information and performing research
3. Formulating a hypothesis (an educated guess)
4. Designing an experiment
5. Analyzing the results
6. Drawing a conclusion

Skill 1.2   **Recognizing and evaluating methods and criteria for collecting, organizing, analyzing, and presenting scientific data**

COLLECTING DATA

The procedure used to obtain data is important to the outcome. Experiments consist of **controls** and **variables**. A control is the experiment run under normal, non-manipulated conditions. A variable is a factor or condition in the experiment that the scientist manipulates. In biology, the variable could be light, temperature, pH, time, etc. Scientists can use the differences in tested variables to make predictions or form hypotheses. Only one variable should be tested at a time. In other words, one would not alter both the temperature and pH of the experimental subject in the same experiment.

An **independent variable** is one the researcher directly changes or manipulates. This could be the amount of light given to a plant or the temperature at which bacteria is grown. The **dependent variable** is the factor that changes as a result of a change in the independent variable.

Data manipulation is important to experimental study. Data manipulation begins by altering one variable at a time, and then assessing the results. Are the results similar to the last time? What has changed? Has the situation assessed by the experiment improved or worsened? This process is part of the scientific method, where scientists make predictions and then experiment to test validity. Quite often, this process takes many alterations, and manipulating the data and experimental parameters is useful. We are fortunate to have technological advances to aid us in this area. Biologists use a variety of tools and technologies to perform tests, collect and display data, and analyze relationships. Examples of commonly used tools include computer-linked probes, spreadsheets, and graphing calculators.

Biologists use computer-linked probes to measure various environmental factors including temperature, dissolved oxygen, pH, ionic concentration, and pressure. The advantage of computer-linked probes, as compared to more traditional observational tools, is that the probes automatically gather data and present it in an accessible format. This eliminates the need for constant human observation and manipulation.

ORGANIZING, ANALYZING, AND DISPLAYING DATA

Tools for Data Organization

Biologists use spreadsheets to organize, analyze, and display data. For example, conservation ecologists use spreadsheets to model population growth and development, apply sampling techniques, and create statistical distributions to analyze relationships. Using spreadsheets simplifies data collection and manipulation and allows the presentation of data in a logical and understandable format.

Graphing programs are another technology with many applications to biology. For example, biologists use algebraic functions to analyze growth, development, and other natural processes. Graphing programs can manipulate algebraic data and create graphs for analysis and observation. In addition, biologists use the matrix function of graphing programs to model problems in genetics. The use of graphing programs simplifies the creation of graphical displays, including histograms, scatter plots, and line graphs. Finally, biologists connect computer-linked probes, used to collect data, to graphing programs to ease the collection, transmission, and analysis of data.
While it is useful to manipulate data in discovery efforts, it is never acceptable to fabricate or falsely advertise your data.

Data Interpretation

When interpreting data, one must carefully examine all parameters. You could be attempting to interpret your own data, or to understand data you found in a published format. Either way, it is important to think about what you see. In the scientific realm, numbers are stronger than words, so be sure to provide accurate data and examples to support your comments.

By using the scientific method, you will be more likely to catch mistakes, correct biases, and obtain accurate results. When assessing experimental data, utilize proper tools and mathematical concepts. Because people often attempt to use scientific evidence to support political or personal agendas, the ability to evaluate the credibility of scientific claims is a necessary skill in today's society.

When evaluating scientific claims made in the media, public debates, and advertising, one should follow several guidelines. First, scientific, peer-reviewed journals are the most accepted source for information on scientific experiments and studies. One should carefully scrutinize any claim that does not reference peer-reviewed literature. Second, the media and those with an agenda to advance (e.g., advertisers and debaters) often overemphasize the certainty and importance of experimental results. One should question any scientific claim that sounds either too good to be true or overly certain. Finally, knowledge of experimental design and the scientific method is important for evaluating the credibility of studies. For example, one should look for the inclusion of control groups and the presence of data to support the given conclusions.

Displaying and presenting data

The type of graphic representation used to display observations depends on the type of data collected. **Line graphs** compare different sets of related data and help predict data. For example, a line graph could compare the rate of activity of different enzymes at varying temperatures. A **bar graph** or **histogram** compares different items and helps make comparisons between or among them based on the data. For example, a bar graph could compare the ages of children in a classroom. A **pie chart** is useful when organizing data as part of a whole. For example, a pie chart could display the percent of time students spend on various after-school activities.

As previously noted, the researcher controls the independent variable. The independent variable is placed on the x-axis (horizontal axis) of a graph. The dependent variable is influenced by the independent variable and is placed on the y-axis (vertical axis) of a graph. It is important to choose the appropriate units for labeling the axes. It is best to divide the largest value to be plotted by the number of blocks on the graph, and round to the nearest whole number.

Also see Skill 4.2.

Skill 1.3   Recognizing and evaluating sources of scientific information (e.g., professional journals, Web sites), their characteristics, and their use

Numerous sources of information are available to instructors and students. Extreme care should be taken to present only validated scientific theory in the classroom; instructors must relentlessly purge incorrect opinions or ideas from instructional presentations, because errors presented as fact in a classroom tend to persist in student memory. Commonly held but erroneous ideas in particular should be addressed, so that students' understanding is based on fact and not popular misconception. An example of this type of erroneous popular thinking is the so-called "fact" that humans use only some minor percentage of their total brain. Ideas like this are not only misleading but actually damaging to a full understanding of the biological sciences.

Hearsay and anecdotal evidence—*which includes personal experiences*—should be treated as irrelevant to a rigorous course of study. Personal experiences may be interesting and personally meaningful, but they do not constitute scientific investigation. Instructors should instead rely only on rigorously tested data, preferably teaching only theory that is widely accepted and well documented. Peer-reviewed journals, textbooks published by reputable companies, and governmentally furnished information should be used in preference to all other sources. Pet theories or popular sciences should not be taught as factual in the classroom. Reputable scientific documentation will have extensive endnotes, citations, and references. In particular, established peer-reviewed journals such as *Science*, *Nature*, and *Scientific American* should be relied upon in preference to Web sites of unknown provenance.

Skill 1.4   Demonstrating familiarity with tools, equipment, and materials commonly used in life science investigations

Light microscopes are commonly used in high school laboratory experiments. Total magnification is determined by multiplying the magnification of the ocular and objective lenses. Oculars usually magnify 10X and objective lenses usually magnify 10X on low and 40X on high.

Procedures for the care and use of microscopes include:

- Cleaning all lenses with lens paper only
- Carrying microscopes with two hands (one on the arm and one on the base)
- Always beginning on low power when focusing before switching to high power
- Storing microscopes with the low power objective down
- Always using a coverslip when viewing wet mount slides
- Bringing the objective down to its lowest position, and then focusing, moving up to avoid breaking the slide or scratching the lens

Wet mount slides should be made by placing a drop of water on the specimen and then putting a glass coverslip on top of the drop of water. Dropping the coverslip at a forty-five degree angle will help avoid air bubbles.

Chromatography refers to a set of techniques that are used to separate substances based on their different properties, such as size or charge. Paper chromatography uses the principles of capillarity to separate substances like plant pigments. Molecules of a larger size will move more slowly up the paper, whereas smaller molecules will move more quickly, producing lines of pigment.

An **indicator** is any substance used to assist in the classification of another substance. An example of an indicator is litmus paper. Litmus paper is a way to measure whether a substance is acidic or basic. Blue litmus turns pink when acid is placed on it, and pink litmus turns blue when a base is placed on it. PH paper is a more accurate measure of pH; this paper turns different colors, depending on the pH value of the substance with which it comes into contact.

Spectrophotometers measure the percent of light at different wavelengths absorbed and transmitted by a pigment solution.

Centrifugation involves spinning substances at a high speed. The denser part of a solution will settle to the bottom of the test tube, whereas the lighter material will stay on top. Centrifugation is used to separate blood into blood cells and plasma, with the heavier blood cells settling to the bottom.

Electrophoresis uses the electrical charges of molecules to separate them according to their size. The molecules, such as DNA or proteins, are pulled through a gel towards either the positive end of the gel box (if the material has a negative charge) or the negative end of the gel box (if the material has a positive charge). DNA is negatively charged and moves towards the positive charge. Smaller segments of DNA will move more quickly toward the positive charge than larger segments.

Skill 1.5   Demonstrating knowledge of practices for ensuring a safe environment in classroom, laboratory, and field settings

GENERAL SAFETY

All laboratory solutions should be prepared as directed in the lab manual. Care should be taken to avoid contamination. All glassware should be rinsed thoroughly with distilled water before using and cleaned well after use. All solutions should be made with distilled water, because tap water contains dissolved particles that can affect the results of an experiment. Unused solutions should be disposed of according to local disposal procedures.

The "Right to Know Law" and Hazardous Chemicals

The "Right to Know Law" covers science teachers who work with potentially hazardous chemicals. Briefly, the law states that employees must be informed of potentially toxic chemicals. An inventory must be made available if requested. The inventory must contain information about the hazards and properties of the chemicals. This inventory is to be checked against the "Substance List." Training must be provided on safe handling and interpretation of the Material Safety Data Sheet.

The following chemicals are potential carcinogens and are not allowed in school facilities: Acrylonitrile, Arsenic compounds, Asbestos, Benzidine, Benzene, Cadmium compounds, Chloroform, Chromium compounds, Ethylene oxide, Ortho-toluidine, Nickel powder, and Mercury.

Chemicals should not be stored on bench tops or heat sources. They should be stored in groups based on their reactivity with one another and in protective storage cabinets. All containers within the lab must be labeled. Suspected and known carcinogens must be labeled as such and stored in trays to contain leaks and spills.

Chemical waste should be disposed of in properly labeled containers. Waste should be separated based on its reactivity with other chemicals.

Biological material should never be stored near food or water intended for human consumption. All biological material should be appropriately labeled. All blood and body fluids should be put in a well-sealed container with a secure lid to prevent leaking. All biological waste should be disposed of in biological hazardous waste bags.

Material safety data sheets are available for every chemical and biological substance. These are available directly from the distribution company and also on the internet. Before using lab equipment, all lab workers should read and understand the equipment manuals.

Safety Equipment

All science labs should contain the following safety equipment:

- Fire blanket that is visible and accessible
- Ground Fault Circuit Interrupters (GFCI) within two feet of water supplies
- Signs designating room exits
- Emergency shower providing a continuous flow of water
- Emergency eye wash station that can be activated by the foot or forearm
- Eye protection for every student
- A means of sanitizing equipment
- Emergency exhaust fans providing ventilation to the outside of the building
- Master cut-off switches for gas, electric, and compressed air. Switches must have permanently attached handles. Cut-off switches must be clearly labeled.

- An ABC fire extinguisher
- Storage cabinets for flammable materials
- Chemical spill control kit
- Fume hood with a motor that is spark-proof
- Protective laboratory aprons made of flame-retardant material
- Signs that will alert of potential hazardous conditions
- Labeled containers for broken glassware, flammables, corrosives, and waste

Safety Procedures for Students

Students should wear safety goggles when performing dissections, heating, or while using acids and bases. Hair should always be tied back and objects should never be placed in the mouth. Food should not be consumed while in the laboratory. Hands should always be washed before and after laboratory experiments. In case of an accident, eye washes and showers should be used for eye contamination or a chemical spill that covers the student's body. Small chemical spills should only be contained and cleaned by the teacher. Kitty litter or a chemical spill kit should be used to clean a spill. For large spills, the school administration and the local fire department should be notified. Biological spills should only be handled by the teacher. Contamination with biological waste can be cleaned by using bleach when appropriate. Accidents and injuries should always be reported to the school administration and local health facilities. The severity of the accident or injury will determine the course of action.

Teacher Responsibilities

It is the responsibility of the teacher to provide a safe environment for his or her students. Proper supervision greatly reduces the risk of injury, and a teacher should never leave a class for any reason without providing alternate supervision. After an accident, two factors are considered: **foreseeability** and **negligence**. Foreseeability is the anticipation that an event might occur under certain circumstances. Negligence is the failure to exercise ordinary or reasonable care. Safety procedures should be a part of the science curriculum, and a well-managed classroom is crucial to avoid potential lawsuits.

Skill 1.6	Applying knowledge of ethics and safety guidelines to the acquisition, care, handling, and disposal of living organisms and to the collection of scientific specimens and data

Few things will repel a student from the biological sciences more than observing an instructor botch a pith of an organism. Instructors should be fully versed and professional in all operations involving living organisms, particularly those with the potential to cause pain or harm to the experimental subject. While dissection offers good education to a certain class of students, below the college level it is generally deemed unnecessary.

Care should be taken to avoid compelling or even overly-encouraging students to participate in classroom activities to which they may object. The most useful type of instruction involving living organisms places the organism in the role of teacher and demonstrates a biological principle with the organism acting in a routine way. Care must be exercised in the acquisition, handling, and disposal of living organisms. Instructors must comply with ethical practices, school system regulations, and especially applicable laws (every jurisdiction presents a complex suite of laws governing these practices).

Additionally, see Skill 1.2 for a discussion of the acquisition of scientific data, and Skill 3.6 for a discussion of scientific ethics.

COMPETENCY 002   **UNDERSTAND APPLICATIONS OF MATHEMATICS AND COMPUTERS IN LIFE SCIENCE**

Skill 2.1   **Applying mathematical concepts and representations (e.g., algebra, equations, graphs) to model and solve quantitative problems in life science and to communicate solutions in a logical and organized manner**

SCIENCE AND TECHNOLOGY

Biological science is closely connected to other scientific disciplines and technology, resulting in a tremendous impact on society and everyday life. Scientific discoveries often lead to technological advances. Conversely, technology is often necessary for scientific investigation, and advances in technology often expand the reach of scientific discoveries. In addition, biology and the other scientific disciplines share several concepts and processes that help unify the study of science. Finally, because biology is the science of living systems, it directly affects society and everyday life.

Science and technology, while distinct concepts, are closely related. Science attempts to investigate and explain the natural world, while technology attempts to solve human adaptation problems. Technology often results from the application of scientific discoveries, and advances in technology can increase the impact of scientific discoveries. For example, Watson and Crick used science to discover the structure of DNA, and their discovery led to many biotechnological advances in the field of genomics. These technological advances greatly influenced the medical and pharmaceutical fields. The success of Watson and Crick's experiments, however, was dependent on the technology available. Without the necessary technology, the experiments would have failed.

The combination of biology and technology has improved the human standard of living in many ways. However, the impact of increasing human life expectancy and the resulting overpopulation on the environment is problematic. In addition, advances in biotechnology (e.g., genetic engineering, cloning) produce ethical dilemmas that society must consider.

CONCEPTS AND PROCESSES

The following are the concepts and processes generally recognized as common to all scientific disciplines:

- Systems, order, and organization
- Evidence, models, and explanation
- Constancy, change, and measurement
- Evolution and equilibrium
- Form and function

Because the natural world is so complex, the study of science involves the **organization** of items into smaller groups based on interaction or interdependence. These groups are called **systems**. Examples of organization are the periodic table of elements and the five-kingdom classification scheme for living organisms. Examples of systems are the solar system, cardiovascular system, Newton's laws of force and motion, and the laws of conservation.

Order refers to the behavior and measurability of organisms and events in nature. The arrangement of planets in the solar system and the life cycle of bacterial cells are examples of order.

Scientists use **evidence** and **models** to form **explanations** of natural events. Models are miniaturized representations of larger events or systems. Evidence is anything that furnishes proof.

Constancy and **change** describe the observable properties of natural organisms and events. Scientists use different systems of **measurement** to observe change and constancy. For example, the freezing and melting points of a given substance and the speed of sound are constant under constant conditions. Growth, decay, and erosion are all examples of natural change.

Evolution is the process of change over a long period of time. While biological evolution is the most common example, one can also classify technological advancement, changes in the universe, and changes in the environment as evolution.

Equilibrium is the state of balance between opposing forces of change. Homeostasis and ecological balance are examples of equilibrium.

Form and **function** are properties of organisms and systems that are closely related. The function of an object usually dictates its form, and the form of an object usually facilitates its function. For example, the form of the heart (e.g., muscle, valves) allows it to perform its function of circulating blood through the body.

Skill 2.2   **Using statistics (e.g., mean, standard deviation, chi-square, linear regression, correlation) to describe and analyze experimental and theoretical data**

Statistics, the rigorous science of collection, organization, and interpretation of data, provides the only acceptable methodology of reporting experimental results in aggregate form. Without robust statistical analysis, any experimental result is simply anecdotal. The statistical methods utilized must be applicable to the data set under observation. Descriptive statistical methods summarize population data numerically and graphically. **Descriptive statistics** include measurements of mean, median, standard deviation, and so forth. **Inferential statistics** use patterns in existing data to predict or deduce facts about the population from which the data were drawn. Inferential statistics seek to establish estimates, correlation, regression, extrapolation, interpolation, and so forth. In general, inferential statistics are more complex than descriptive statistics, but this is not always true.

Some well-known and broadly accepted statistical methods include chi-square, regression analysis, and correlation. The processes for performing these analyses are widely available in any introductory statistics textbook, and any statistics package will support these and other methods.

Skill 2.3   Demonstrating knowledge of applications of computers in life science (e.g., designing models, selecting appropriate software and hardware)

Models are often the basis for greater understanding. Models are usually small-scale representations that help us understand larger systems. Models aid us by making unusually large or small items more concrete. Common models include the solar system and the DNA helix; more complex models include computer simulations of complicated systems. It is important to note that models are created with information. How current and accurate the information is at the time of the model's creation can make the model more or less useful later. For example, although Pluto has been considered a planet for many years, it is now considered a dwarf planet. This is due to the progressive nature of science; the more we learn, the more we are forced to reevaluate.

COMPETENCY 003   **UNDERSTAND THE CONTENT AND METHODS FOR DEVELOPING STUDENTS' CONTENT-AREA READING SKILLS TO SUPPORT THEIR READING AND LEARNING IN LIFE SCIENCE**

Skill 3.1   **Demonstrating knowledge of key components and processes involved in reading (e.g., vocabulary knowledge, including orthographic and morphological knowledge; background knowledge; knowledge of academic discourse, including the syntactic and organizational structures used in print and digital academic texts; print processing abilities, including decoding skills; use of cognitive and metacognitive skills and strategies)**

Science is a body of knowledge systematically derived from study, observations, and experimentation. The objective of science is to identify and establish principles and theories that are utilized to solve problems. Pseudoscience, on the other hand, involves beliefs that are not supported by hard evidence. In other words, there is no scientific methodology or application in pseudoscience. Some classic examples of pseudoscience include witchcraft, alien encounters, or any topic explained by hearsay.

Scientific experimentation must be repeatable. Experimentation results in theories that can be disproved and changed. Science depends on communication, as well as both agreement and disagreement among scientists. It is composed of theories, laws, and hypotheses.

A theory is a statement of principles or relationships relating to a natural event or phenomenon, which has been verified and accepted.

A law is an explanation of events that occur with uniformity under the same conditions (e.g., laws of nature, law of gravitation).

A hypothesis is an unproved theory or educated guess, followed by research, to best explain a phenomenon. A theory is a proven hypothesis.

Science is limited by the currently available technology. An example of this would be the relationship between the discovery of the cell and the invention of the microscope. As technology improves, more hypotheses will become theories and possibly laws. Data collection methods also limit scientific inquiry. Data might be interpreted differently on different occasions. The inherent limitations of scientific methodology produce results or explanations that are subject to change as new technologies emerge.

Facts are not always as finite as they appear. More commonly in science, information is a hypothesis or, once tested and confirmed, a theory. Theories exist for long periods of time and are repeatedly challenged. Only when a theory has withstood every challenge and been proven to provide reproducible results does it become recognized as a law. It is this universal recognition that defines a theory as a scientific law.

A **concept** is a general understanding or belief. Scientists challenge concepts. The purpose of the scientific method is to derive clear, unbiased data. Concepts, on the other hand, can be fraught with personal biases and gray areas, overly simplistic, or too encompassing. A scientist might examine a concept, and then try to confirm it by making and testing a hypothesis. In this way, scientific inquiry is more specific than concepts.

Skill 3.2	**Demonstrating ability to plan instruction and select strategies that support all students' content-area reading (e.g., differentiating instruction to meet the needs of students with varying reading proficiency levels and linguistic backgrounds, identifying and addressing gaps in students' background knowledge, scaffolding reading tasks for students who experience comprehension difficulties)**

Classroom teaching involves the ability to plan instruction and select strategies that support the needs of all students. Not every student learns best via the same route as others. Typical methodologies used in classroom teaching include, but are not limited to:

- Explaining, similar to lecturing
- Modeling, where visual aids are used alongside other teaching methods
- Demonstrating, in which processes are demonstrated during storytelling of the process; this method works particularly well with simple experimentation
- Collaborating, in which students work in groups, which can be short-lived or long-lived, depending on the need and teaching goals
- Discussion, where students are allowed open discussion of ideas, opinion, and bias; care must be taken to guide the discussion into constructive areas
- Learning by teaching, where students are asked to instruct other students

All of these methods and others can be effective for some students. One method should not be used to the exclusion of all others, however, or else the instruction will become routine and ineffective.

Skill 3.3	**Demonstrating knowledge of explicit strategies for facilitating students' comprehension before, during, and after reading content-area texts and for promoting students' use of comprehension strategies**

Students must be taught comprehension strategies. Simple tools such as summarizing after every paragraph of reading have been demonstrated to increase comprehension. Typical strategies of teaching comprehension are to encourage frequent summarization, ask questions, answer questions, and foster cooperative learning. Graphic organization of content helps some students visualize and comprehend difficult or complex topics. Continuously monitoring comprehension ability is a foundational principle of any specific strategy. Comprehension can be gauged by examination or by discussion. Modern teaching practices often utilize specific, defined comprehension programs that seek to encompass all of these goals while simultaneously producing meaningful metrics.

Most students learn best when new topics build on prior knowledge. This helps them relate new ideas to existing ideas that are well understood. Fortunately, biology lends itself quite well to this type of incremental introduction of new and difficult topics.

Students should be given a toolbox of comprehension strategies including things like questioning, summarizing, visualizing, evaluating, and synthesizing new ideas. Students do not arrive with a readymade toolbox, however; they must be taught how to learn.

Skill 3.4   **Demonstrating knowledge of explicit strategies for promoting students' academic language and vocabulary development, including their knowledge of domain-specific vocabulary words**

The average person's active vocabulary probably consists of some 10,000 words. The biological sciences introduce perhaps three to four dozen new words per major topic. This means that a typical biology course will introduce something on the order of 500 to1,000 new words, each of which has a specific meaning. Students must thus increase their vocabulary by approximately 5-10% to accommodate the science of biology.

Such a task is not trivial, even for motivated students. Instructors must adapt a formal and well-defined strategy of vocabulary development to successfully teach biology. Testing should take vocabulary into account, though exams should not become simply excursions into vocabulary definition. Students should be provided with standardized definitions of terms, almost universally available in textbook glossaries, and instructors must be fully familiar with the terms used and their precise meanings. This is especially true of words that have colloquial or common meanings that are different from their biological meanings, such as energy, metabolism, respiration, organic, and so forth. If the instructor's vocabulary usage is lackadaisical, or terms are used in the classroom inconsistently, students will become confused.

Skill 3.5   **Demonstrating knowledge of explicit strategies for developing students' critical literacy skills (e.g., encouraging students to question texts, developing students' ability to analyze texts from multiple viewpoints or perspectives)**

Biology instruction is a part of the students' overall educational process. The primary focus must be on biological topics, but methodologies should be used to enhance students' critical literary skills. Students should be encouraged to read critically, to examine conclusions and statistics carefully, and to attempt to analyze new ideas from a variety of viewpoints and perspectives. To accomplish this, classroom discussion and collaboration are particularly useful. Again, care must be taken to ensure these types of activities stay on meaningful topics and are constructive. Students should learn that different opinions and experiences are not incorrect, but simply different. Instructors should incorporate approved methodologies for fostering critical skill development into lesson plans and teaching methods.

Skill 3.6   Demonstrating ability to plan instruction and select strategies that support students' reading and understanding of life science texts (e.g., helping students to relate what is read to relevant prior knowledge, to follow laboratory activity instructions, and to interpret diagrams and graphs in terms of scientific content or meaning)

LESSON PLANS

Lesson plans detail and describe the course of instruction for a particular class period's activities. The plan should address how the topic will be taught, the subject being covered, and desired outcomes. Plans must incorporate requirements mandated by the school system. The best lesson plans should incorporate a sequencing, a time estimate, lists of required materials, a list of objectives, an introductory statement, the instruction component to be taught, some method of independent assessment, a wrap-up summary, and a continuity component that springboards into the subsequent lesson plan. If it is appropriate, lesson plans can also contain an evaluation component. Good lesson plans will include some type of analysis component, which will allow instructors to review the lesson plan based on real-world experience and perform updates so the same plan will function better the next time it is used.

Successful lesson plans should address the interests and educational needs of students and incorporate best-practices from current educational theory. Typically, several lesson plans are put into sequence to form the basics of a larger unit plan; often evaluation components are handled at the unit plan level. Lesson and unit plans help instructors to remain focused on specific objectives within defined timelines.

Assignments

Assignments should vary so that students do not become bored or produce rote work. Assignments can involve one student, a group of students, or perhaps the entire class. They can involve individual learning or group learning. Assignments must realistically allow adequate time for students to complete work. Assignments should focus student attention on the desired outcomes of the teaching topic, and should be detailed in the lesson plan. There is an extensive body of literature addressing learning plan development and assignment construction theory.

SCIENTIFIC ETHICS

To understand scientific ethics, we need to have a clear understanding of general ethics. Ethics is a system of public, general rules that guide human conduct. The rules are general because they apply to all people at all times, and they are public because they are not secret codes or practices.

The following are some of the guiding principles of scientific ethics:

1. Scientific Honesty: Refrain from fabricating or misinterpreting data for personal gain.
2. Caution: Avoid errors and sloppiness in all scientific experimentation.
3. Credit: Give credit where credit is due and do not copy.
4. Responsibility: Report reliable information to the public and do not mislead in the name of science.
5. Freedom: Freedom to criticize old ideas, question new research, and conduct independent research.

Scientists should show good conduct in their scientific pursuits. Conduct here refers to all aspects of scientific activity, including experimentation, testing, education, data evaluation, data analysis, data storing, and peer review.

DOMAIN II   MOLECULAR AND CELLULAR LIFE PROCESSES

COMPETENCY 004   UNDERSTAND CELLULAR STRUCTURES AND
                   PROCESSES

Skill 4.1   Recognizing organelles and other cellular structures, their
              characteristics and functions, and the interactions between
              organelles and other cellular structures

TYPES OF CELLS

The cell is the basic unit of all living things. There are three types of cells:
archaea, prokaryotic, and eukaryotic. Archaea have some similarities with prokaryotes,
but are as distantly related to prokaryotes as prokaryotes are to eukaryotes.

Archaea

There are three kinds of organisms with archaea cells: **methanogens**, obligate
anaerobes that produce methane; **halobacteria**, which can live only in concentrated
brine solutions; and **thermoacidophiles**, which can live only in acidic hot springs.

Prokaryotes

Prokaryotes consist only of bacteria and cyanobacteria (formerly known as blue-green
algae). The diagram below depicts the classification of prokaryotes.

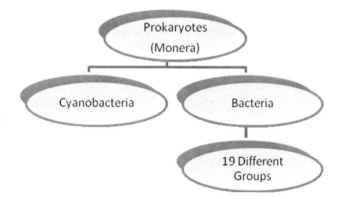

Bacterial cells have no defined nucleus or nuclear membrane. The DNA, RNA, and
ribosomes float freely within the cell. The cytoplasm has a single chromosome
condensed to form a **nucleoid**. All prokaryotes have a thick cell wall made up of amino
sugars (glycoproteins) that provides protection, gives the cell shape, and keeps the cell
from bursting. The antibiotic penicillin targets the **cell wall** of bacteria. Penicillin works
by disrupting the cell wall, thus killing the cell.

The cell wall surrounds the **cell membrane** (plasma membrane). The cell membrane consists of a lipid bilayer that controls the passage of molecules in and out of the cell. Some prokaryotes have a capsule, made of polysaccharides, surrounding the cell wall for extra protection from higher organisms.

Many bacterial cells have appendages called **flagella** that are used for movement. Some cells also have **pili**, which are a protein strand used for attachment. Pili are also used for sexual conjugation, during which bacterial cells exchange DNA.

Prokaryotes are the most numerous and widespread organisms on earth. Bacteria were most likely the first cells, and date back in the fossil record to 3.5 billion years ago. Their ability to adapt to the environment allows them to thrive in a wide variety of habitats.

Eukaryotes

Eukaryotic cells are found in protists, fungi, plants, and animals. Most eukaryotic cells are larger than prokaryotic cells. They contain many **organelles**, which are membrane-bound areas for specific functions. Their cytoplasm contains a cytoskeleton, which provides a protein framework for the cell. The cytoplasm also supports the organelles and contains the ions and molecules necessary for cell function. The cytoplasm is contained by the plasma membrane. The plasma membrane allows molecules to pass in and out of the cell. The membrane can bud inward to engulf outside material in a process called endocytosis. Exocytosis is a secretory mechanism, the reverse of endocytosis.

Elements and structure of eukaryotic cells

The most significant differentiation between prokaryotes and eukaryotes is that eukaryotes have a **nucleus**. The nucleus is the "brain" of the cell that contains all of the cell's genetic information. The chromosomes consist of chromatin, which are complexes of DNA and proteins. The chromosomes are tightly coiled to conserve space while providing a large surface area. The nucleus is the site of transcription of the DNA into RNA. The **nucleolus** is where ribosomes are made. There is at least one of these dark-staining bodies inside the nucleus of most eukaryotes. The nuclear envelope consists of two membranes separated by a narrow space. The envelope contains many pores that let RNA out of the nucleus.

Ribosomes are the site for protein synthesis. Ribosomes can be free-floating in the cytoplasm or attached to the endoplasmic reticulum. There may be up to a half a million ribosomes in a cell, depending on how much protein the cell makes.

The **endoplasmic reticulum** (ER) is folded and has a large surface area. It is the "roadway" of the cell and allows for transport of materials through and out of the cell. There are two types of ER: smooth and rough. Smooth endoplasmic reticulum does not contain ribosomes on the surface and is the site of lipid synthesis. Rough endoplasmic reticulum has ribosomes on its surface and aids in the synthesis of proteins that are membrane-bound or destined for secretion.

Many of the products made in the ER proceed to the Golgi apparatus. The **Golgi apparatus** sorts, modifies, and packages molecules that are made in other parts of the cell (like the ER). These molecules are sent either out of the cell or to other organelles within the cell.

Lysosomes are found mainly in animal cells. These contain digestive enzymes that break down food, unnecessary substances, viruses, damaged cell components, and, eventually, the cell itself. It is believed that lysosomes play a role in the aging process.

Mitochondria are large organelles that are the site of cellular respiration, the process of ATP production that supplies energy to the cell. Muscle cells have many mitochondria because they use a great deal of energy. Mitochondria have their own DNA, RNA, and ribosomes, and are capable of reproducing by binary fission if there is a great demand for additional energy. Mitochondria have two membranes: a smooth outer membrane and a folded inner membrane. The folds inside the mitochondria are called **cristae**. They provide a large surface area for cellular respiration to occur.

Plastids are found only in photosynthetic organisms. They are similar to mitochondria in that they both have a double membrane structure. They also have their own DNA, RNA, and ribosomes, and can reproduce if the need for the increased capture of sunlight becomes necessary. There are several types of plastids. **Chloroplasts** are the site of photosynthesis. The stroma is the chloroplast's inner membrane space. The stroma encloses sacs called thylakoids that contain the photosynthetic pigment **chlorophyll**. The chlorophyll traps sunlight inside the thylakoid to generate ATP, which is used in the stroma to produce carbohydrates and other products. The **chromoplasts** make and store yellow and orange pigments. They provide color to leaves, flowers, and fruits. The **amyloplasts** store starch and are used as a food reserve. They are abundant in roots like potatoes.

The **Endosymbiotic Theory** states that mitochondria and chloroplasts were once free-living and possibly evolved from prokaryotic cells. At some point in evolutionary history, they entered the eukaryotic cell and maintained a symbiotic relationship with the cell. The fact that they have their own DNA, RNA, and ribosomes, and are capable of reproduction, supports this theory.

Found only in plant cells, the **cell wall** is composed of cellulose and fibers. It is thick enough for support and protection, yet porous enough to allow water and dissolved substances to enter.

Vacuoles are found mostly in plant cells. They hold stored food and pigments. Their large size allows them to fill with water in order to provide turgor pressure. Lack of turgor pressure causes a plant to wilt.

The **cytoskeleton**, found in both animal and plant cells, is composed of protein filaments attached to the plasma membrane and organelles. The cytoskeleton provides a framework for the cell and aids in cell movement. Three types of fibers make up the cytoskeleton:

1. **Microtubules**: The largest of the three fibers, they make up cilia and flagella for locomotion. Some examples are sperm cells, cilia that line the fallopian tubes, and tracheal cilia. Centrioles are also composed of microtubules. They aid in cell division to form the spindle fibers that pull the cell apart into two new cells. Centrioles are not found in the cells of higher plants.
2. **Intermediate filaments**: Intermediate in size, they are smaller than microtubules, but larger than microfilaments. They help the cell keep its shape.
3. **Microfilaments**: Smallest of the three fibers, they are made of actin and small amounts of myosin (like in muscle tissue). They function in cell movement like cytoplasmic streaming, endocytosis, and amoeboid movement. This structure pinches the two cells apart after cell division, forming two new cells.

The following is a diagram of a generalized animal cell.

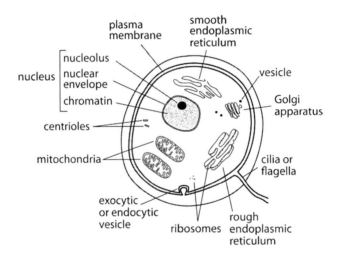

Skill 4.2 **Demonstrating knowledge of methods of measurement used to describe cellular structures and physiological processes**

Math, science, and technology share many common themes. All three use models, diagrams, and graphs to simplify concepts for analysis and interpretation. Patterns observed in these systems lead to predictions based on these observations. Another common theme among these three systems is equilibrium. **Equilibrium** is a state in which forces are balanced, resulting in stability. Static equilibrium is stability due to a lack of changes, and dynamic equilibrium is stability due to a balance between opposing forces.

MEASUREMENT

Science uses the **metric system**, because it is accepted worldwide and allows the results of experiments, performed by different scientists around the world, to be compared to one another. The meter is the basic metric unit of length. One meter is equal to 1.1 yards. The liter is the basic metric unit of volume. 3.846 liters is equal to 1 gallon. The gram is the basic metric unit of mass. One thousand grams is equal to 2.2 pounds. The following prefixes define multiples of the basic metric units:

Prefix	Multiplying factor	Prefix	Multiplying factor
deca-	10X the base unit	deci-	1/10 the base unit
hecto-	100X	centi-	1/100
kilo-	1,000X	milli-	1/1,000
mega-	1,000,000X	micro-	1/1,000,000
giga-	1,000,000,000X	nano-	1/1,000,000,000
tera-	1,000,000,000,000X	pico-	1/1,000,000,000,000

Instruments of Measurement

The most common instrument used for measuring volume is the graduated cylinder. The standard unit of measurement is milliliters (mL). To ensure accurate measurement, it is important to read the liquid in the cylinder at the bottom of the meniscus, the curved surface of the liquid.

The most common instrument used in measuring mass is the triple-beam balance. The triple-beam balance can accurately measure tenths of a gram and can estimate hundredths of a gram.

The ruler and meter stick are the most commonly used instruments for measuring length. As with all scientific measurements, standard units of length are metric.

Cellular structures are invisible to the unaided eye and, for the most part, cannot directly be measured. Instead, various types of microscopes are utilized. Optical microscopes may be used with a variety of laboratory measurement devices that often are placed in the frame of view and magnified alongside the subject. Electron microscopes use a variety of sophisticated techniques to obtain accurate measurements of various objects within cells. Most physiological processes are measured as a rate per unit time, and they may be averaged or reported as a series of instantaneous values with, for example, a graph.

Skill 4.3	Analyzing how cells respond to changes in their environment to maintain homeostasis (e.g., active transport, exocytosis)

Cells use a variety of mechanisms to respond to their environment and maintain homeostasis. A primary activity of cells is the import or export of chemicals such as food, water, oxygen, carbon dioxide, and waste products. Excretory cells also excrete products such as hormones or lipoproteins.

Active transport is used when a cell must move chemicals against their concentration gradient. This type of transport uses energy and can be accomplished in a variety of ways. Passive transport is used when cells must move chemicals down their concentration gradient. This type of transport does not use energy, but in some cases can be directly controlled by the cell. For large-scale importation or exportation of bulk chemicals or objects, cells may use phagocytosis, a type of cellular membrane budding process. The membrane can bud inward to engulf outside material in a process called endocytosis. Exocytosis is a secretory mechanism, the reverse of endocytosis.

Skill 4.4 Demonstrating knowledge of the cellular processes of a given plant or animal cell (e.g., guard cell, muscle cell, phagocyte)

Multi-cellular organisms are comprised of a variety of specialized cells that perform a given task by the selective enabling of genes. For example, guard cells surround the stoma of plant leaves and control the ingress or egress of gasses. If the plant is losing too much water through transpiration, the guard cells will close the stoma, thus trapping all water vapor within the leaf's waxy cuticle. Once temperatures drop or more water becomes available, the guard cells will open the stoma, allowing fresh atmosphere, rich in carbon dioxide, to perfuse the interior tissue of the leaf.

Muscle cells are contractile and are structured so their length can be shortened by the exertion of energy. Numerous muscle cells are fused into a single, long, multi-nucleate cell with enhanced strength and length. Muscle fibers consist of multiple such muscle cells joined together in long strands. Under nervous system control, the muscle fibers can contract because the muscle cells can contract individually.

In humans, phagocytes are a class of large immune system cells that roam tissues and seek foreign bodies or proteins, which are ingested and destroyed through enzymatic action. Note that, in all of these examples, the cell's structure is specialized to match the cell's function. In addition to performing a specialized service, all of these cells constant undergo the routine functions of all living cells; specifically, they metabolize energy and maintain homeostasis.

COMPETENCY 005   **UNDERSTAND PHOTOSYNTHESIS AND CELLULAR RESPIRATION**

Skill 5.1   **Analyzing the structure of chloroplasts and how structure and function are related**

See Skill 5.2.

Skill 5.2   **Demonstrating knowledge of the processes involved in the transformation of solar energy into cellular energy, including biochemical pathways (e.g., Calvin cycle) and electron transport**

Photosynthesis is an anabolic process that stores energy in the form of a three-carbon sugar. We will use glucose as an example for this section.

ORGANISMS THAT PERFORM PHOTOSYNTHESIS

Photosynthesis occurs only in organisms that contain chloroplasts (i.e., plants, some bacteria, and some protists). There are a few terms to be familiar with when discussing photosynthesis.

An **autotroph** (self-feeder) is an organism that makes its own food from the energy of the sun or other elements. Autotrophs include:

- **Photoautotrophs**: Organisms that make food from light and carbon dioxide, releasing oxygen that can be used for respiration.
- **Chemoautotrophs**: Organisms that oxidize sulfur and ammonia. Some bacteria are chemoautotrophs.

Heterotrophs (other feeder) are organisms that must eat other living things to obtain energy. Another term for heterotrophs is **consumers**. All animals are heterotrophs.

Decomposers break down once living things. Bacteria and fungi are examples of decomposers. **Scavengers** eat dead things. Examples of scavengers are bacteria, fungi, and some animals.

PROCESS OF PHOTOSYNTHESIS

The **chloroplast** is the site of photosynthesis in a plant cell. Similar to mitochondria in a eukaryotic cell, chloroplasts contain an increased surface area of membrane called the thylakoid membrane. The thylakoid membrane contains pigments (chlorophyll) that are capable of capturing light energy. Between the membranous stacks of thylakoids there is a fluid called stroma.

Photosynthesis reverses the electron flow. Water is split by the chloroplast into hydrogen and oxygen. Oxygen is released as a waste product while carbon dioxide is reduced to sugar (glucose). This requires the input of energy, which comes from the sun.

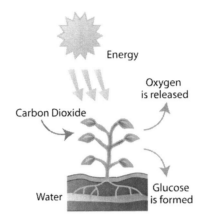

Stages of Photosynthesis

Photosynthesis occurs in two stages, the light reactions and the Calvin cycle (dark reactions). The conversion of solar energy to chemical energy occurs during light reactions. In light reactions, chlorophyll absorbs light and uses the energy to split water, releasing oxygen as a waste product. Light energy that has been converted to chemical energy is stored in the form of NADPH and ATP. Both NADPH and ATP are then used in the Calvin cycle to produce sugar.

The second stage of photosynthesis is the **Calvin cycle**. Carbon dioxide in the air is incorporated into organic molecules already in the chloroplast. The NADPH produced in the light reaction is used as reducing power for the reduction of the carbon to carbohydrate. ATP from the light reaction is also needed to convert carbon dioxide to carbohydrate (sugar).

The two stages of photosynthesis are summarized below.

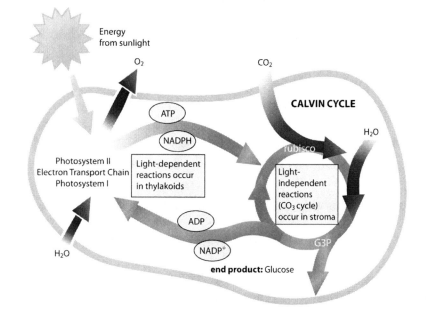

The Role of the Sun in Photosynthesis

The process of photosynthesis is made possible by the sun. Visible light ranges in wavelengths of 750 nanometers (red light) to 380 nanometers (violet light). As the wavelength decreases, the amount of available energy increases. Light is carried as photons, which are fixed quantities of energy. Light is reflected (what we see), transmitted, or absorbed (what the plant uses). The plant's pigments capture light of specific wavelengths. Remember that the reflected light is what we see as color. Plant pigments include:

- Chlorophyll *a*: Reflects green/blue light; absorbs red light
- Chlorophyll *b*: Reflects yellow/green light; absorbs red light
- Carotenoids: Reflects yellow/orange light; absorbs violet/blue light

The pigments absorb photons. The energy from the light excites electrons in the chlorophyll that jump to orbitals with more potential energy and reach an "excited" or unstable state.

The Chemical Process of Photosynthesis

The formula for photosynthesis is:

$$CO_2 + H_2O + \text{energy (from sunlight)} \rightarrow C_6H_{12}O_6 \text{ (glucose)} + O_2$$

The high-energy electrons are trapped by primary electron acceptors, which are located on the thylakoid membrane. These electron acceptors and the pigments form reaction centers called photosystems that are capable of capturing light energy. Photosystems contain a reaction-center chlorophyll that releases an electron to the primary electron acceptor. This transfer is the first step of the light reactions. There are two photosystems, named according to their dates of discovery, not their order of occurrence.

1. **Photosystem I** is composed of a pair of chlorophyll *a* molecules. Photosystem I is also called P700 because it absorbs light of 700 nanometers. Photosystem I makes ATP, the energy from which energy is needed to build glucose.
2. **Photosystem II** is also called P680 because it absorbs light of 680 nanometers. Photosystem II produces ATP + $NADPH_2$ and the waste gas oxygen.

Both photosystems are bound to the **thylakoid membrane**, close to electron acceptors.

The production of ATP is termed **photophosphorylation** due to the use of light. Photosystem I uses cyclic photophosphorylation because the pathway occurs in a cycle. It can also use noncyclical photophosphorylation, which starts with light and ends with glucose. Photosystem II uses noncyclical photophosphorylation only.

Below is a diagram of the relationship between photosynthesis and cellular respiration, which will be covered in the following section.

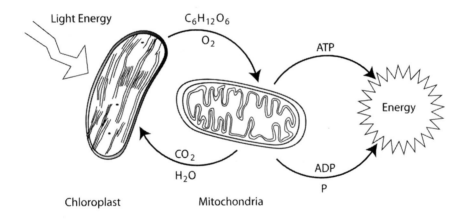

Skill 5.3   Analyzing the structure of mitochondria and how structure and function are related

See Skill 5.4.

Skill 5.4 **Demonstrating knowledge of the processes involved in the release of energy stored in food molecules during cellular respiration, including biochemical pathways (e.g., glycolysis, Krebs cycle) and ATP synthesis**

Cellular respiration is the metabolic pathway in which food (e.g., glucose) is broken down to produce energy in the form of ATP. Both plants and animals utilize respiration to create energy for metabolism. In respiration, energy is released by the transfer of electrons in a process known as an **oxidation-reduction (redox)** reaction. The oxidation phase of this reaction is the loss of an electron and the reduction phase is the gain of an electron. Redox reactions are important for all stages of respiration.

PROCESS OF CELLULAR RESPIRATION

Glycolysis is the first step in respiration. It occurs in the cytoplasm of the cell and does not require oxygen. Each of the ten stages of glycolysis is catalyzed by a specific enzyme. The following is a summary of these stages.

Ten Stages of Glycolysis

In the first stage, the reactant is glucose. For energy to be released from glucose, it must be converted to a reactive compound. This conversion occurs through the phosphorylation of a molecule of glucose by the use of two molecules of ATP. This is an investment of energy by the cell. The 6-carbon product, called fructose -1,6-bisphosphate, breaks into two 3-carbon molecules of sugar. A phosphate group is added to each sugar molecule and hydrogen atoms are removed. Hydrogen is picked up by NAD^+ (a vitamin). Because there are two sugar molecules, two molecules of NADH are formed. The reduction (addition of hydrogen) of NAD allows the potential for energy transfer.

As the phosphate bonds are broken, ATP is produced. Two ATP molecules are generated as each original 3-carbon sugar molecule is converted to pyruvic acid (pyruvate). A total of four ATP molecules are made in the four stages. Because two molecules of ATP are needed to start the reaction in stage 1, there is a net gain of two ATP molecules at the end of glycolysis. This accounts for only two percent of the total energy in a molecule of glucose.

The Krebs Cycle

Beginning with pyruvate, which was the end product of glycolysis, the following steps occur before entering the **Krebs cycle**.

1. Pyruvic acid is changed to acetyl-CoA (coenzyme A). This is a 3-carbon pyruvic acid molecule, which has lost one molecule of carbon dioxide (CO_2) to become a 2-carbon acetyl group. Pyruvic acid loses a hydrogen atom to NAD^+, which is reduced to NADH.

2. Acetyl CoA enters the Krebs cycle. For each molecule of glucose with which it started, two molecules of Acetyl CoA enter the Krebs cycle (one for each molecule of pyruvic acid formed in glycolysis).

The **Krebs cycle** (also known as the citric acid cycle), occurs in four major steps. First, the 2-carbon acetyl CoA combines with a 4-carbon molecule to form a 6-carbon molecule of citric acid. Next, two carbons are lost as carbon dioxide (CO_2) and a 4-carbon molecule is formed, which is available to join with CoA to form citric acid again. Because we started with two molecules of CoA, two turns of the Krebs cycle are necessary to process the original molecule of glucose. In the third step, eight hydrogen atoms are released and picked up by FAD and NAD (vitamins and electron carriers).

Lastly, for each molecule of CoA (remember, there were two at the beginning) you get:

- 3 molecules of NADH x 2 cycles
- 1 molecule of $FADH_2$ x 2 cycles
- 1 molecule of ATP x 2 cycles

Therefore, this completes the breakdown of glucose. At this point, a total of four molecules of ATP have been made, two from glycolysis and one from each of the two turns of the Krebs cycle. Six molecules of carbon dioxide have been released, two prior to entering the Krebs cycle and two for each of the two turns of the Krebs cycle. Twelve carrier molecules have been made, ten NADH and two $FADH_2$. These carrier molecules will carry electrons to the electron transport chain.

The Electron Transport Chain

ATP is made by substrate level phosphorylation in the Krebs cycle. Notice that the Krebs cycle in itself does not produce many ATP molecules. Instead, it functions mostly for the transfer of electrons that are subsequently used in the electron transport chain to generate large numbers of ATP molecules. In the **Electron Transport Chain**, NADH transfers electrons from glycolysis and the Krebs cycle to the first molecule in the chain of molecules embedded in the inner membrane of the mitochondrion.

Most of the molecules in the electron transport chain are proteins. Nonprotein molecules are also part of the chain, and are essential for the catalytic functions of certain enzymes. The electron transport chain does not make ATP directly. Instead, it breaks up a large free energy drop into a more manageable one. The chain uses electrons to pump H^+ ions across the mitochondrial membrane. The H^+ gradient is used to form ATP synthesis in a process called **chemiosmosis** (oxidative phosphorylation). ATP synthetase and energy, generated by the movement of hydrogen ions coming from NADH and $FADH_2$, builds ATP from ADP on the inner membrane of the mitochondria.

Each NADH yields three molecules of ATP (10 x 3) and each $FADH_2$ yields two molecules of ATP (2 x 2). Thus, the electron transport chain and oxidative phosphorylation produces 34 ATP, and the net gain from the whole process of respiration is 36 molecules of ATP.

Process	# ATP produced (+)	# ATP consumed (-)	Net # ATP
Glycolysis	4	2	+2
Acetyl CoA	0	2	-2
Krebs cycle	1 per cycle (2 cycles)	0	+2
Electron transport chain	34	0	+34
Total			+36

AEROBIC VERSUS ANAEROBIC RESPIRATION

q

Glycolysis generates ATP with oxygen (aerobic) or without oxygen (anaerobic). We have already discussed aerobic respiration. Anaerobic respiration occurs through fermentation. In the process of fermentation, ATP is generated by substrate level phosphorylation if enough NAD^+ is present to accept electrons during oxidation. In anaerobic respiration, NAD^+ is regenerated by transferring electrons to pyruvate. There are two common types of fermentation.

Types of Fermentation

In **alcoholic fermentation**, pyruvate is converted to ethanol in two steps. In the first step, carbon dioxide is released from the pyruvate. In the second step, ethanol is produced when acetaldehyde is reduced by NADH. This results in the regeneration of NAD^+ for glycolysis. Alcohol fermentation is carried out by yeast and some bacteria.

In **lactic acid fermentation**, pyruvate is reduced by NADH forming lactate as a waste product. Animal cells and some bacteria that do not use oxygen utilize lactic acid fermentation to make ATP. Lactic acid forms when pyruvic acid accepts hydrogen from NADH. A buildup of lactic acid is what causes muscle soreness following exercise.

Differences between Aerobic and Anaerobic Respiration

Energy remains stored in lactic acid or alcohol until it is needed. This is not an efficient type of respiration. When oxygen is present, aerobic respiration occurs after glycolysis.

Both aerobic and anaerobic pathways oxidize glucose to pyruvate through the process of glycolysis and both pathways employ NAD^+ as an oxidizing agent. A substantial difference between the two pathways is that in fermentation, an organic molecule such as pyruvate or acetaldehyde is the final electron acceptor. In respiration, the final electron acceptor is oxygen. Another key difference is that respiration yields much more energy from a sugar molecule than fermentation does. Respiration can produce up to 18 times more ATP than fermentation.

Skill 5.5 **Applying knowledge of structure-function relationships and the relationships between organelles and the cellular environment to predict the effect of a given physical or chemical change (e.g., light intensity, pH) on photosynthesis or cellular respiration**

Organelles respond appropriately to changes in the environment. For example, when light intensity increases, the chloroplasts begin photosynthesis; if the inputs to photosynthesis are not available, the chloroplast might change predominantly to cyclic electron flow or even photorespiration. When the inputs become available again, the chloroplast might change predominantly to non-cyclic electron flow.

Similarly, when oxygen is not present, cellular respiration will change to anaerobic processes such as fermentation, and the mitochondria will cease electron transport chain activities. A review of photosynthesis (Skill 5.2) and cellular respiration (Skill 5.4) will help illuminate the link between the structure and function of the organelles involved.

COMPETENCY 006   **UNDERSTAND THE STRUCTURE AND FUNCTION OF PROTEINS AND THE PROCESS OF PROTEIN SYNTHESIS**

Skill 6.1   Identifying the basic chemical composition and structure of proteins

A compound consists of two or more elements. There are four major chemical compounds found in the cells and bodies of living things. These are carbohydrates, lipids, proteins, and nucleic acids.

Monomers are the simplest unit of structure. **Monomers** combine to form **polymers**, or long chains, making a large variety of molecules. Monomers combine through the process of condensation reactions (also called dehydration synthesis). In this process, one molecule of water is removed from between each of the adjoining molecules. In order to break the molecules apart in a polymer, water molecules are added between monomers, thus breaking the bonds between them. This process is called hydrolysis.

Proteins comprise about fifty percent of the dry weight of animals and bacteria. Proteins function in:

- Structure and support (e.g., connective tissue, hair, feathers, and quills)
- Storage of amino acids (e.g., albumin in eggs and casein in milk)
- Transport of substances (e.g., hemoglobin)
- Coordination of body activities (e.g., insulin)
- Signal transduction (e.g., membrane receptor proteins)
- Contraction (e.g., muscles, cilia, and flagella)
- Body defense (e.g., antibodies)
- As enzymes to speed up chemical reactions

All proteins are made of twenty **amino acids**. An amino acid contains an amino group and an acid group. The radical group varies and defines the amino acid. Amino acids form through condensation reactions that remove water. The bond formed between two amino acids is called a **peptide bond**. Polymers of amino acids are called polypeptide chains. An analogy can be drawn between the twenty amino acids and the alphabet. We can form millions of words using an alphabet of only twenty-six letters. Similarly, organisms can create many different proteins using the twenty amino acids. This results in the formation of many different proteins, the structures of which typically defines their function.

There are four levels of protein structure: primary, secondary, tertiary, and quaternary.

1. **Primary structure** is the protein's unique sequence of amino acids. A slight change in primary structure can affect a protein's conformation and its ability to function.

2. **Secondary structure** is the coils and folds of polypeptide chains. The coils and folds are the result of hydrogen bonds along the polypeptide backbone. The secondary structure is either in the form of an alpha helix or a pleated beta sheet. The alpha helix is a coil held together by hydrogen bonds. A pleated beta sheet is the polypeptide chain folding back and forth. The hydrogen bonds between parallel regions hold it together.

3. **Tertiary structure** results from bonds between the side chains of the amino acids. For example, disulfide bridges form when two sulfhydryl groups on the amino acids form a strong covalent bond.

4. **Quaternary structure** is the overall structure of the protein from the aggregation of two or more polypeptide chains. An example of this is hemoglobin. Hemoglobin consists of two kinds of polypeptide chains.

Skill 6.2 Demonstrating knowledge of the processes of transcription and translation, including the roles of DNA and RNA

See Skill 9.1.

Skill 6.3 Predicting the amino acid sequence of a protein from a given codon sequence

DNA is read in base pair triplets called **codons**. Each base pair has one of four possible values, so there are 4 * 4 * 4 = 64 possible codons. Each codon "codes" for a specific amino acid. Because there are more codons than amino acids, several codons might code for the same amino acid. Some codons have additional meanings, such as "start" and "stop" of a gene; ATG signifies a "start" and the several "stop" codons are noted in the table below. The following table is a typical representation of the various codons and the amino acids that they represent. This table shows DNA codons; a similar table could be constructed to show RNA codons.

			2nd base						
			T		**C**		**A**		**G**
1st base	**T**	TTT	(Phe/F) Phenylalanine	TCT	(Ser/S) Serine	TAT	(Tyr/Y) Tyrosine	TGT	(Cys/C) Cysteine
		TTC	(Phe/F) Phenylalanine	TCC	(Ser/S) Serine	TAC	(Tyr/Y) Tyrosine	TGC	(Cys/C) Cysteine
		TTA	(Leu/L) Leucine	TCA	(Ser/S) Serine	TAA	Ochre (*Stop*)	TGA	Opal (*Stop*)
		TTG	(Leu/L) Leucine	TCG	(Ser/S) Serine	TAG	Amber (*Stop*)	TGG	(Trp/W) Tryptophan
	C	CTT	(Leu/L) Leucine	CCT	(Pro/P) Proline	CAT	(His/H) Histidine	CGT	(Arg/R) Arginine
		CTC	(Leu/L) Leucine	CCC	(Pro/P) Proline	CAC	(His/H) Histidine	CGC	(Arg/R) Arginine
		CTA	(Leu/L) Leucine	CCA	(Pro/P) Proline	CAA	(Gln/Q) Glutamine	CGA	(Arg/R) Arginine
		CTG	(Leu/L) Leucine	CCG	(Pro/P) Proline	CAG	(Gln/Q) Glutamine	CGG	(Arg/R) Arginine
	A	ATT	(Ile/I) Isoleucine	ACT	(Thr/T) Threonine	AAT	(Asn/N) Asparagine	AGT	(Ser/S) Serine
		ATC	(Ile/I) Isoleucine	ACC	(Thr/T) Threonine	AAC	(Asn/N) Asparagine	AGC	(Ser/S) Serine

		ATA	(Ile/I) Isoleucine	ACA	(Thr/T) Threonine	AAA	(Lys/K) Lysine	AGA	(Arg/R) Arginine
G		ATG	(Met/M) Methionine	ACG	(Thr/T) Threonine	AAG	(Lys/K) Lysine	AGG	(Arg/R) Arginine
		GTT	(Val/V) Valine	GCT	(Ala/A) Alanine	GAT	(Asp/D) Aspartic acid	GGT	(Gly/G) Glycine
		GTC	(Val/V) Valine	GCC	(Ala/A) Alanine	GAC	(Asp/D) Aspartic acid	GGC	(Gly/G) Glycine
		GTA	(Val/V) Valine	GCA	(Ala/A) Alanine	GAA	(Glu/E) Glutamic acid	GGA	(Gly/G) Glycine
		GTG	(Val/V) Valine	GCG	(Ala/A) Alanine	GAG	(Glu/E) Glutamic acid	GGG	(Gly/G) Glycine

To use the table, observe the individual base pairs of the codon—for example, CAG. Read the first base pair down the left-hand column; read the second base pair across the top row. The resulting intersection will have four entries, so find the entry ending with the third base pair to resolve the codon to its amino acid. In this example, CAG codes for Glutamine. Even though all polypeptides initially begin with methionine, this amino acid can later be stripped off during post-translational processing.

Skill 6.4 Recognizing the functions of proteins, including enzymes, in living organisms and factors that affect protein function

Enzymes act as biological catalysts that speed up reactions. Enzymes are the most diverse type of protein. They are not used up in a reaction and are recyclable. Each enzyme is specific for a single reaction. Enzymes act on a substrate, which is the material to be broken down or put back together. Most enzymes end in the suffix -*ase* (lipase, amylase). The prefix is the substrate being acted on (lipids, sugars).

$$\text{Substrate} \xrightarrow{\text{Enzyme}} \text{Product}$$

The active site is the region of the enzyme that binds to the substrate. There are two theories for how the active site functions. The **lock and key theory** states that the shape of the enzyme is specific because it fits into the substrate like a key fits into a lock. According to this theory, the enzyme holds molecules close together so reactions can easily occur. The **induced fit theory** states that an enzyme can stretch and bend to fit the substrate. This is the most accepted theory.

Many factors can affect enzyme activity. Temperature and pH are two such factors. The temperature can affect the rate of reaction of an enzyme. The optimal pH for enzymes is between 6 and 8, with a few enzymes' optimal pH falling outside of this range.

Cofactors aid in the enzyme's function. Cofactors can be inorganic or organic. Organic cofactors are known as coenzymes. Vitamins are examples of coenzymes. Some chemicals can inhibit an enzyme's function. **Competitive inhibitors** block the substrate from entering the active site of the enzyme to reduce productivity. **Noncompetitive**

inhibitors bind to a location on the enzyme that is different from the active site and interrupts substrate binding. In most cases, noncompetitive inhibitors alter the shape of the enzyme. **Allosteric enzymes** can exist in two shapes; they are active in one form and inactive in the other. Overactive enzymes can cause metabolic diseases.

Also see Skill 6.1.

DOMAIN III   MOLECULAR REPRODUCTION AND HEREDITY

COMPETENCY 007 UNDERSTAND THE PROCESSES OF MITOSIS AND MEIOSIS

Skill 7.1   Recognizing stages of the cell cycle and factors that affect the division and growth of cells

The purposes of cell division are to provide growth and repair in body (somatic) cells and to replenish or create sex cells for reproduction. There are two forms of cell division: mitosis and meiosis. **Mitosis** is the division of somatic cells and **meiosis** is the division of sex cells (eggs and sperm).

MITOSIS

Phases of Mitosis

Mitosis is divided into two parts: the **mitotic (M) phase** and **interphase**. In the mitotic phase, mitosis and cytokinesis divide the nucleus and cytoplasm, respectively. The mitotic phase is the shortest phase of the cell cycle. Interphase is the stage during which the cell grows and copies the chromosomes in preparation for the mitotic phase. Interphase occurs in three stages of growth: the G_1 (growth) period, when the cell grows and metabolizes; the **S** (synthesis) period, when the cell makes new DNA; and the G_2 (growth) period, when the cell makes new proteins and organelles in preparation for cell division.

The mitotic phase is a continuum of change, although it is divided into five distinct stages: prophase, prometaphase, metaphase, anaphase, and telophase.

Stages of the mitotic phase

During **prophase**, the cell proceeds through the following steps continuously, without stopping. First, the chromatin condenses to become visible chromosomes. Next, the nucleolus disappears and the nuclear membrane breaks apart. Then, mitotic spindles, composed of microtubules, form. These will eventually pull the chromosomes apart. Finally, the cytoskeleton breaks down and the centrioles push the spindles to the poles, or opposite ends of the cell.

During **prometaphase**, the nuclear membrane fragments and allows the spindle microtubules to interact with the chromosomes. Kinetochore fibers attach to the chromosomes at the centromere region.

Metaphase begins when the centrosomes are at opposite ends of the cell. The centromeres of all the chromosomes are aligned with one another.

During **anaphase**, the centromeres split in half and homologous chromosomes separate. The chromosomes are pulled to the poles of the cell, with identical sets at either end.

The last stage of mitosis is **telophase**. During this phase, two nuclei form, each with a full set of DNA that is identical to that of the parent cell. The nucleoli become visible and the nuclear membrane reassembles. A cell plate is seen in plant cells and a cleavage furrow forms in animal cells. The cell pinches into two cells. Finally, cytokinesis, or division of the cytoplasm and organelles, occurs.

Below is a diagram of mitosis.

Mitosis

Interphase		x number of chromosomes
Prophase		chromosomes double (2x) and crossover
Prometaphase		nucleus dissolves and microtubules attach to centromeres
Metaphase		chromosomes align at middle of cell
Anaphase		separated chromosomes pull apart
Telophase		microtubules disappear cell division begins
Cytokinesis		2 cells formed each with x chromosomes

Skill 7.2   Recognizing the characteristics and behavior of chromosomes in eukaryotic cells

Eukaryotic chromosomes have well-understood activities that transpire throughout cell division. DNA is normally found as chromatin, or a dispersed form, during cell growth. During mitosis and meiosis, the DNA condenses into dense coiled bodies called chromosomes. The alignment and division of chromosomes defines the various phases of mitosis and meiosis.

See Skill 7.1 for information about mitosis and Skill 7.4 for information about meiosis.

Skill 7.3   Demonstrating knowledge of changes in the visibility, arrangement, and number of chromosomes in the various stages of mitosis and meiosis

The visibility, arrangement, and number of chromosomes in the various stages of mitosis and meiosis are fully described in Skill 7.1 and Skill 7.4, respectively. Under ordinary circumstances, the only time a human cell will have an odd number of chromosomes is during meiosis, when the haploid count is n = 23. For this reason, classroom demonstrations often focus on human chromosome counts.

Skill 7.4   Analyzing how meiosis and fertilization contribute to genetic variability

MEIOSIS

Meiosis is similar to mitosis, but there are two consecutive cell divisions, meiosis I and meiosis II, in order to reduce the chromosome number by one-half. This way, when the sperm and egg join during fertilization, the diploid number is reached.

Phases of Meiosis

Similar to mitosis, meiosis is preceded by an interphase, during which the chromosome replicates. The steps of meiosis are as follows:

1. **Prophase I**: The replicated chromosomes condense and pair with homologues in a process called synapsis. This forms a tetrad. Crossing over, the exchange of genetic material between homologues to further increase diversity, occurs during prophase I.
2. **Metaphase I**: The homologous pairs attach to spindle fibers after lining up in the middle of the cell.
3. **Anaphase I**: The sister chromatids remain joined and move to the poles of the cell.
4. **Telophase I**: The homologous chromosome pairs continue to separate. Each pole now has a haploid chromosome set. Telophase I occurs simultaneously with cytokinesis. In animal cells, a cleavage furrow forms, and, in plant cells, a cell plate appears.
5. **Prophase II**: A spindle apparatus forms and the chromosomes condense.
6. **Metaphase II**: Sister chromatids line up in center of cell. The centromeres divide and the sister chromatids begin to separate.
7. **Anaphase II**: The separated chromosomes move to opposite ends of the cell.
8. **Telophase II**: Cytokinesis occurs, resulting in four haploid daughter cells.

Below is a diagram of meiosis:

Meiosis

Interphase	x number of chromosomes
Prophase	chromosomes double (2x) and crossover
Prometaphase	nucleus dissolves and microtubules attach to centromeres
Metaphase I	chromosomes align at middle of cell
Anaphase I	separated chromosomes pull apart
Telophase I	microtubules disappear cell division begins
Prophase II	2 cells formed each with x chromosomes
Metaphase II	microtubules attach to centromeres
Anaphase II	chromosomes pull apart
Telophase II	microtubules disappear cell division begins
Cytokinesis	4 cells form each with half the number of original chromosomes ($\frac{1}{2} x$)

Labels in diagram: nucleus, chromosomes, centrioles, spindle fibers

Skill 7.5 Applying knowledge of the characteristics of chromosomes and the laws of segregation and independent assortment to explain how sex is determined in humans

During meiosis, human males (XY) will produce haploid gametes (sperm); roughly 50% of these gametes will contain an "X" chromosome and the other 50% will contain a "Y" chromosome. During meiosis, human females (XX) will produce haploid games (egg); all of these gametes will contain an "X" chromosome. During fertilization, two possibilities arise: An "X" sperm will fuse with an "X" egg, resulting in a female (XX) zygote, or a "Y" sperm will fuse with an "X" egg, resulting in a male (XY) zygote.

It can thus be seen that sex determination in humans is fairly straightforward, and because only the male can donate a "Y" chromosome, it is often said that "the father determines the baby's sex". Because human males are XY, they are subject to sex-linked genetic disease with greater frequency than females (in other words, human males cannot be heterozygous for sex-linked traits). See Skill 8.4 for more information. Note that, although numerous other species use the "XY" system of sex determination, it is not universal.

COMPETENCY 008   UNDERSTAND THE CONCEPTS AND PRINCIPLES OF HEREDITY

Skill 8.1   Demonstrating knowledge of how traits are inherited and expressed

HISTORY OF GENETICS

Gregor Mendel is recognized as the father of genetics. His work in the late 1800s is the basis of our knowledge of genetics. Although unaware of the presence of DNA or genes, Mendel realized there were factors (now known as **genes**) that were transferred from parents to their offspring. Mendel worked with pea plants and fertilized the plants himself, keeping track of subsequent generations, which led to the Mendelian laws of genetics. Mendel found that two "factors" governed each trait, one from each parent. Traits or characteristics came in several forms, known as **alleles**. For example, the trait of flower color had white alleles (*pp*) and purple alleles (*PP*). Mendel formulated two laws: the law of segregation and the law of independent assortment.

LAWS OF GENETICS

Law of Segregation

The **law of segregation** states that only one of the two possible alleles from each parent is passed on to the offspring. If the two alleles differ, then one is fully expressed in the organism's appearance (the dominant allele) and the other has no noticeable effect on appearance (the recessive allele). The two alleles for each trait segregate into different gametes. A **Punnett square** can be used to show the law of segregation. In a Punnett square, one parent's genes are put at the top of the box and the other parent's are put on the side. Genes combine in the squares just like numbers are added in addition tables. This Punnett square shows the result of the cross of two F_1 hybrids.

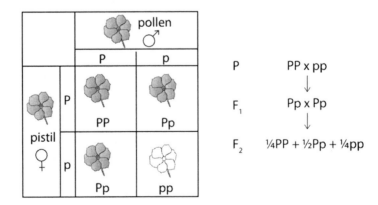

This cross results in a 1:2:1 ratio of F_2 offspring. Here, the *P* is the dominant allele and the *p* is the recessive allele. The F_1 cross produces three offspring expressing the dominant allele (one *PP* and two *Pp*) and one offspring expressing the recessive allele (*pp*).

The following are some other important terms to know:

- **Homozygous**: Having a pair of identical alleles. For example, *PP* and *pp* are homozygous pairs.
- **Heterozygous**: Having two different alleles. For example, *Pp* is a heterozygous pair.
- **Phenotype**: The organism's physical appearance
- **Genotype**: The organism's genetic makeup. For example, *PP* and *Pp* have the same phenotype (purple in color), but different genotypes.

Law of Independent Assortment

The **law of independent assortment** states that alleles assort independently of each other. The law of segregation applies to monohybrid crosses (only one character, in this case, flower color, is the variable in the experiment). In a dihybrid cross, two characters are explored. Two of the seven characters Mendel studied were seed shape and color. Yellow is the dominant seed color (*Y*), and green is the recessive color (*y*). The dominant seed shape is round (*R*), and the recessive shape is wrinkled (*r*). A cross between a plant with yellow round seeds (*YYRR*) and a plant with green wrinkled seeds (*yyrr*) produces an F_1 generation with the genotype *YyRr*. Independent assortment of the *YyRr* genotype yields four possible outcomes (*YR*, *Yr*, *yR*, and *yr*). Crossing the F_1 generation would result in the production of F_2 offspring with a 9:3:3:1 phenotypic ratio.

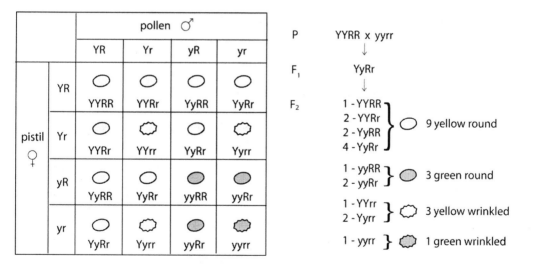

Dominance

Based on Mendelian genetics, the more complex hereditary pattern of **dominance** was discovered. In Mendel's law of segregation, the F_1 generation has either purple or white flowers. This is an example of **complete dominance**. **Incomplete dominance** occurs when the F_1 generation results in an appearance somewhere between the two parents. For example, red flowers are crossed with white flowers, resulting in an F_1 generation with pink flowers. The red and white traits are still carried by the F_1 generation, resulting in an F_2 generation with a phenotypic ratio of 1:2:1. In **codominance,** the genes can form new phenotypes.

ABO blood grouping is an example of codominance. A and B are of equal strength and O is recessive. Therefore, type A blood may have the genotypes of AA or AO, type B blood may have the genotypes of BB or BO, type AB blood has the genotype A and B, and type O blood has two recessive O genes.

Pedigrees

A family pedigree is a collection of a family's history for a particular trait. As you work your way through a pedigree of interest, Mendelian inheritance theories are applied. In tracing a trait, the generations are mapped in a pedigree chart, similar to a family tree but with the alleles present. In a case where both parents have a particular trait and one of two children also expresses this trait, the trait is due to a dominant allele. In contrast, if both parents do not express a trait and one of their children does, that trait is due to a recessive allele.

Non-Mendelian Inheritance

Non-Mendelian inheritance is a general term describing any pattern of genetic inheritance that does not conform to Mendel's laws or does not rely on a single chromosomal gene. Examples of non-Mendelian inheritance include complex traits, environmental influence, organelle DNA, transmission bias, and epigenetics.

Complex traits

Multiple genes determine the expression of many complex traits. For example, disorders arising from a defect in a single gene are rare compared to complex disorders like cancer, heart disease, and diabetes. The inheritance of such complex disorders does not follow Mendelian rules because it involves more than one gene.

Organelle DNA

While chromosomal DNA carries the majority of an organism's genetic material, organelles, including mitochondria and chloroplasts, also have DNA containing genes. Organelle genes have their own patterns of inheritance that do not conform to Mendelian rules. Such patterns of inheritance are often called maternal, because offspring receive all of their organelle DNA from the mother.

Transmission bias

Transmission bias describes a situation in which the alleles of the parent organisms are not equally represented in their offspring. Transmission bias often results from the failure of alleles to segregate properly during cell division. Mendelian genetics assumes equal representation of parent alleles in the offspring generation.

Epigenetics

Epigenetic inheritance involves changes that do not involve DNA sequence. For example, the addition of methyl groups (methylation) to DNA molecules can influence the expression of genes and override Mendelian patterns of inheritance.

Genetic linkage

Finally, genetic linkage, discussed in detail in the next section, is often considered a form of non-Mendelian inheritance because closely linked chromosomal genes tend to assort together, not separately. Linkage, however, is not entirely non-Mendelian, because classical genetics can generally explain and predict the patterns of inheritance of linked traits.

Skill 8.2   Recognizing evidence that a particular characteristic is inherited

Lacking evidence to the contrary, it can be assumed that phenotypic characteristics are inherited. Any trait within a species that is diagnostic of the species is inherited. Even highly variable traits (in humans, traits such as eye color, skin color, and hair color) are most likely inherited. Even acquired traits (such as muscle development in bodybuilders) have at least a basis in inheritable genetics. Especially when controlled mating is possible, traits can be determined to be inherited by constructing pedigrees and utilizing other genetic techniques.

Skill 8.3   Demonstrating knowledge of the application of statistical analyses for describing the results from a given plant or animal breeding experiment

Using Mendel's principles, as discussed in Skill 8.1, it is fairly easy to construct probability matrices for traits that follow Mendelian inheritance. Assuming a diploid organism and a single trait, gametes can contain only one of two possible alleles, and fertilization can therefore produce only one of four possible outcomes. Assuming a diploid organism with two traits considered together, gametes can contain only one of four possible allele combinations, and fertilization can therefore produce only sixteen possible genetic outcomes.

In classical Mendelian experiments, a homozygous dominant organism crossed with a homozygous recessive organism will produce a 1:2:1 ratio for a single trait and a 9:3:3:1 ratio for two traits taken together. This type of analysis can be conducted for any number of traits taken simultaneously, but it rapidly becomes unwieldy. This type of probability matrix closely mirrors the Punnett squares described and illustrated in Skill 8.1. Obviously, traits following non-Mendelian inheritance require different statistical methods, but even these traits can be estimated if their inheritance patterns are known.

Skill 8.4 **Applying knowledge of the rules of probability and heredity (e.g., law of independent assortment) to predict the genotypic and phenotypic outcomes of offspring resulting from crosses of parents with given traits, including dominant-recessive, incomplete and co-dominant, polygenic, and sex-linked traits**

Most simple genetic inheritances used in the classroom assume sexually reproducing, diploid organisms, and focus on one or two traits at a time. These types of demonstrations assume that there is no genetic linkage or other types of skewing or distortion of the law of independent assortment or the law of segregation (see Skill 8.1 for definitions of these laws). Because non-Mendelian genetics work usually involves complex formulae and solid knowledge of the traits in question, non-Mendelian examples are seldom used in the classroom.

Parents with specified traits that follow dominant-recessive inheritance, or incomplete or co-dominant inheritance, are easily demonstrated with a Punnett square, as described and illustrated in Skill 8.1. Human blood type is often used as the typical demonstration of co-dominance. Polygenic inheritance can also be demonstrated with a Punnett square, but care must be taken to note the various genetic inputs and track them appropriately. The typical polygenic inheritance model demonstrated in the classroom deals with a continuously variable trait such as human height.

Sex-linked traits follow a straightforward but slightly modified process of inheritance, and can easily be demonstrated with modified Punnett squares showing the possibilities divided by sex. Traits such as color blindness in humans or eye color in fruit flies are typically used to demonstrate sex-linked inheritance.

COMPETENCY 009   **UNDERSTAND GENETIC MUTATIONS AND FACTORS THAT AFFECT THE EXPRESSION OF GENES**

Skill 9.1   **Recognizing the relationships between DNA, genes, and chromosomes**

TRANSLATION

Proteins are synthesized through the process of **translation**. Three major classes of RNA are needed to carry out these processes: messenger RNA (mRNA), ribosomal RNA (rRNA), and transfer RNA (tRNA). **Messenger RNA** contains information for translation. **Ribosomal RNA** is a structural component of the ribosome, and **transfer RNA** carries amino acids to the ribosome for protein synthesis.

Transcription

Transcription is similar in prokaryotes and eukaryotes. During transcription, the DNA molecule is copied into an RNA molecule (mRNA). Transcription occurs through the steps of initiation, elongation, and termination. Transcription also occurs for rRNA and tRNA, but the focus here is on mRNA.

Stages of transcription

Initiation begins at the promoter of the double-stranded DNA molecule. The promoter is a specific region of DNA that directs the **RNA polymerase** to bind to the DNA. The double-stranded DNA opens up, and RNA polymerase begins transcription in the 5' → 3' direction by pairing ribonucleotides to the deoxyribonucleotides as follows to get a complementary mRNA segment:

Deoxyribonucleotide		Ribonucleotide
A	→	U
G	→	C

Elongation is the synthesis of the mRNA strand in the 5' → 3' direction. The new mRNA rapidly separates from the DNA template, and the complementary DNA strands pair together.

Termination of transcription occurs at the end of a gene. Cleavage occurs at specific sites on the mRNA. This process is aided by termination factors.

Posttranscriptional Processing

In eukaryotes, mRNA goes through **posttranscriptional processing** before going on to translation.

Stages of posttranscriptional processing

There are three basic steps of processing:

1. **5' capping:** The addition of a base with a methyl attached to it that protects the 5' end from degradation and serves as the site where ribosomes bind to the mRNA for translation
2. **3' polyadenylation**: The addition of 100-300 adenines to the free 3' end of mRNA resulting in a poly-A-tail
3. **Intron removal**: The removal of non-coding introns and the splicing together of coding exons form the mature mRNA.

The Translation Process

Translation is the process in which the mRNA sequence becomes a polypeptide. The mRNA sequence determines the amino acid sequence of a protein by following a pattern called the genetic code. The **genetic code** consists of 64 triplet nucleotide combinations called **codons**. Three codons are termination codons, and the remaining 61 code for amino acids. There are 20 amino acids encoded by different mRNA codons. Amino acids are the building blocks of protein. They are attached together by peptide bonds to form a polypeptide chain.

Ribosomes are the site of translation. They contain rRNA and many proteins.

Stages of translation

Translation occurs in three steps: initiation, elongation, and termination.

Initiation occurs when the methylated tRNA binds to the ribosome to form a complex. This complex then binds to the 5' cap of the mRNA.

During elongation, tRNAs carry the amino acid to the ribosome and place it in order according to the mRNA sequence. tRNA is very specific: It only accepts one of the 20 amino acids that correspond to the anticodon. The anticodon is complementary to the codon. For example, using the codon sequence below:

the mRNA reads   A U G / G A G / C A U / G C U
the anticodons are   U A C / C U C / G U A / C G A

Termination occurs when the ribosome reaches any one of the three stop codons: UAA, UAG, or UGA. The newly formed polypeptide then undergoes posttranslational modification to alter or remove portions of the polypeptide.

Skill 9.2 Recognizing different types of mutations (e.g., substitution, deletion) and their effects

Inheritable changes in DNA are called mutations. **Mutations** can be errors in replication or a spontaneous rearrangement of one or more nucleotide segments by factors such as radioactivity, drugs, or chemicals.

The severity of the change is not as critical as where the change occurs. DNA contains large segments of non-coding areas called introns. The important coding areas are called exons. If an error occurs in an intron, it has no effect. If the error occurs in an exon, it can range from having no effect to being lethal, depending on the severity of the mistake.

Mutations can occur on somatic or sex cells. Usually mutations in sex cells are more dangerous, because they contain the blueprint for the developing offspring. However, mutations are not always bad. They are the basis of evolution, and if they create a favorable variation that enhances the organism's survival, they are beneficial. However, mutations can also lead to abnormalities, birth defects, and even death. There are several types of mutations.

TYPES OF MUTATIONS

A **point mutation** is a mutation involving a single nucleotide or a few adjacent nucleotides. Let us suppose a normal sequence was as follows:

Normal	A B C D E F	
Duplication	A B **C C** D E F	one nucleotide is repeated
Inversion	A **E D C B** F	a segment of the sequence is flipped
Deletion	A B C E F	a nucleotide is left out (D is lost)
Insertion	A B C **R S** D E F	nucleotides are inserted or translocated
Breakage	A B C	a piece is lost (DEF is lost)

Deletion and insertion mutations that shift the reading frame are called **frame shift mutations**.

A **silent mutation** alters the nucleotide sequence but does not change the amino acid sequence; therefore, it does not alter the protein.

A **missense mutation** results in an alteration in the amino acid sequence. A mutation's effect on protein function depends on which amino acids are involved and how many are involved. The structure of a protein usually determines its function.

A mutation that does not alter the structure of a protein will probably have little or no effect on the protein's function. However, a mutation that does alter the structure of a protein and severely affects protein activity is called a **loss-of-function mutation**. Sickle-cell anemia and cystic fibrosis are examples of loss-of-function mutations.

Skill 9.3   Demonstrating knowledge of how mutations occur and factors that can cause genetic mutations

Mutations can occur by spontaneous action, such as through hydrolysis of the DNA polymer, or by induced actions from environmental sources. Some chemicals and radiation are known to cause mutations. Several types of viral infection have also been demonstrated to cause genetic mutations. The action of most mutagens is not well understood at the chemical level, but advances are being made. Mutation rates are not constant across species, and some organisms have so-called DNA hotspots where mutations occur at rapid rates.

Exposure to ionizing or nonionizing radiation can cause mutation. Exposure to mutagenic chemicals can also cause mutation. Infection by some viral diseases can cause mutation. Several types of mutation are described in Skill 9.2.

Skill 9.4   Demonstrating knowledge of the control of gene expression in cells

In bacterial cells, the *lac* operon is a good example of the control of gene expression. The *lac* operon contains the genes that code for the enzymes used to convert lactose into fuel (glucose and galactose). The *lac* operon contains three genes, *lac Z*, *lac Y*, and *lac A*. *Lac Z* codes for an enzyme that converts lactose into glucose and galactose. *Lac Y* codes for an enzyme that causes lactose to enter the cell. *Lac A* codes for an enzyme that acetylates lactose.

The *lac* operon also contains a promoter and an operator that is the "off and on" switch for the operon. A protein called the repressor switches the operon off when it binds to the operator. When lactose is absent, the repressor is active and the operon is turned off. The operon is turned on again when allolactose (formed from lactose) inactivates the repressor by binding to it.

Gene expression in eukaryotic cells is much more complicated and involves a series of go/no-go checkpoints. Additionally, the processes of transcription and translation are under complex forms of controls, as discussed in Skill 9.1.

Skill 9.5   Analyzing the effects of environmental changes on the expression of genetic traits

Gene expression can be controlled by environmental factors, as with the *lac* operon in prokaryotic organisms (described in Skill 9.4). Eukaryotic organisms can also have genes that are controlled by environmental changes. Part of basic cellular homeostasis involves maintaining an internal environment that appropriately regulates gene expression.

COMPETENCY 010 **UNDERSTAND THE PROCESSES AND APPLICATIONS OF GENETIC TECHNOLOGY**

Skill 10.1 Recognizing the principles and processes of producing recombinant DNA

Genetic engineering has made enormous contributions to medicine and has enabled significant enhancements in DNA technology.

The use of DNA probes and the polymerase chain reaction (PCR) has enabled scientists to identify and detect elusive pathogens. Diagnosis of genetic disease is now possible before the onset of symptoms.

In its simplest form, genetic engineering requires enzymes to cut DNA, as well as a vector and a host organism in which to place the recombinant DNA. A **restriction enzyme** is a bacterial enzyme that cuts foreign DNA in specific locations. The restriction fragment that results can be inserted into a bacterial plasmid **(vector)**. Other vectors that can be used include viruses and bacteriophages. The splicing of restriction fragments into a plasmid results in a recombinant plasmid. This recombinant plasmid can then be placed in a host cell, usually a bacterial cell, for replication.

The use of recombinant DNA provides a means to transplant genes among species. This opens the door for cloning specific genes of interest. Hybridization can be used to find a gene of interest. A **probe** is a molecule complementary to the sequence of a gene of interest. The probe, once annealed to the gene, can be detected by labeling with a radioactive isotope or a fluorescent tag.

Gel electrophoresis is another method for analyzing DNA. Electrophoresis separates DNA or protein by size or electrical charge. The DNA runs towards the positive charge and the DNA fragments separate by size. The gel is treated with a DNA-binding dye that fluoresces under ultraviolet light. A picture of the gel can be taken and used for analysis.

One of the most widely used genetic engineering techniques is the **polymerase chain reaction (PCR)**. PCR is a technique in which a piece of DNA can be amplified into billions of copies within a few hours. This process requires a primer to specify the segment to be copied, and an enzyme (usually taq polymerase) to amplify the DNA. PCR has allowed scientists to perform multiple procedures on small amounts of DNA.

Skill 10.2 Demonstrating knowledge of applications of genetic technology in the treatment of human diseases

Genetic engineering has allowed for the treatment of some genetic disorders. **Gene therapy** is the introduction of a normal allele into somatic cells to replace a defective allele. The medical field has had success in treating patients with a single enzyme deficiency. Gene therapy has allowed doctors and scientists to introduce a normal allele, which provides the missing enzyme.

Insulin and mammalian growth hormones have been produced in bacteria by gene-splicing techniques. Insulin treatment helps control diabetes for millions of people who suffer from the disease. The insulin produced in genetically engineered bacteria is chemically identical to that made in the pancreas. Human growth hormone (HGH) has been genetically engineered for the treatment of dwarfism caused by insufficient amounts of HGH. HGH is being researched further for the treatment of broken bones and severe burns.

Biotechnology has advanced the techniques used to create vaccines. Genetic engineering allows for the modification of a pathogen in order to attenuate it for vaccine use. In fact, vaccines created by a pathogen attenuated by gene-splicing might be safer than those that use traditional mutants.

Skill 10.3   Demonstrating knowledge of applications of genetic technology in the development of agricultural products

The genetic modification of food crops is widely practiced and often controversial. Common genetic manipulations provide protection from insects, fungi, and virus infection. These genetic modifications are intended to ease crop management, reduce pesticide and fungicide needs, and increase crop yields. Additionally, some crops are genetically modified to grow larger, to be more resistant to drought, temperature, or salinity, or to have enhanced nutritional value. Currently, some crops are being designed to provide specific proteins useful as pharmaceuticals. Ethical and food safety issues are often raised in an attempt to stop or slow the production of genetically modified food crops. Many of the methods discussed in Skill 10.1 are used in the production of genetically modified food crops.

DOMAIN IV   STRUCTURAL AND FUNCTIONAL RELATIONSHIPS

COMPETENCY 011   UNDERSTAND THE CHARACTERISTICS AND
                   PROCESSES OF LIFE AND STRUCTURES OF COMMON
                   ORGANISMS

Skill 11.1   Recognizing characteristics that distinguish living organisms from
              nonliving things and methods and evidence for determining the
              presence of life

Living organisms are distinguished from non-living objects because living organisms:

- Undergo metabolism
- Maintain homeostatis
- Grow
- Respond to stimuli
- Reproduce
- As populations, evolve

Not every living organism exhibits all of these traits, but all living things exhibit most of
these traits.

Skill 11.2   Demonstrating knowledge of structures of representative organisms
              from major taxonomic groups

Several of the major animal phyla are listed below, along with their basic structures and
the common names of representative organisms. Other groups exist in the other
kingdoms of life—for example, Skill 12.1 summarizes some of the major groupings in
kingdom plantae.

Porifera: Sponges; they contain spicules for support. Porifera possess flagella for
movement in the larval stage, but later become sessile and attach to a firm object.
Sponges can reproduce sexually (either by cross- or self-fertilization) or asexually (by
budding). Porifera are filter feeders and digest food by phagocytosis. They require water
to support their hydroskeletons and are therefore mostly aquatic.

Cnidaria (Coelenterata): Jellyfish; these animals possess stinging cells called
nematocysts. They can be found in a sessile polyp form with the tentacles at the top, or
in a moving medusa form with the tentacles floating below. Jellyfish have a
hydroskeleton that requires water for support. They have no true muscles. Cnidaria can
reproduce asexually (by budding) or sexually. They are the first group to possess a
primitive nervous system.

Platyhelminthes: Flatworms; the flat shape of these animals aids in the diffusion of
gases. They are the first group with true muscles. Flatworms can reproduce asexually
(by regeneration) or sexually. Platyhelminthes can be hermaphroditic, possessing both

male and female sex organs, but cannot fertilize themselves. These worms are parasites because they have no true nervous system.

Nematoda: Roundworms; the first animal with a true digestive system with a separate mouth and anus. Roundworms can be parasites or simple consumers. Nematoda reproduce sexually with male and female worms. They possess longitudinal muscles and thrash about when they move.

Mollusca : Cams, octopus; the soft-bodied animals. These animals have a muscular foot for movement. They breathe through gills, and most are able to make a shell for protection from predators. They have an open circulatory system with sinuses that bathe the body regions.

Annelida: Segmented worms; the first group with specialized tissue. The advanced circulatory system of these worms has blood vessels and is a closed system. The nephridia are their excretory organs. Annelida are hermaphroditic, and each worm fertilizes the other during mating. Segmented worms support themselves with a hydrostatic skeleton and have circular and longitudinal muscles for movement.

Arthropoda: Insects, crustaceans, and spiders; this is the largest group of the animal kingdom. Phylum arthropoda accounts for about 85% of all the animal species. Arthropoda possess an exoskeleton made of chitin. They must molt to grow. They breathe through gills, trachea, or book lungs. Movement varies; members are able to swim, fly, and crawl. There is a division of labor among the appendages (legs, antennae, etc). This is an extremely successful phylum; its members occupy diverse habitats.

Echinodermata: Sea urchins and starfish; these animals have spiny skin. Their habitat is marine. They have tube feet for locomotion and feeding.

Chordata: All animals with a notocord or a backbone. The classes in this phylum include Agnatha (jawless fish), Chondrichthyes (cartilage fish), Osteichthyes (bony fish), Amphibia (frogs and toads; possess gills that are replaced by lungs during development), Reptilia (snakes, lizards; the first group to lay eggs with a protective covering), Aves (birds; warm-blooded), and Mammalia (animals that do not lay eggs, possess mammary glands that produce milk, and are warm-blooded).

Skill 11.3   Analyzing structural and functional relationships involved in basic life processes (e.g., obtaining nutrients and energy, maintaining homeostasis, reproducing, growing) carried out by organisms from major taxonomic groups

Organisms are comprised of organ systems, which are in turn comprised of organs and tissues. These various systems perform the functions required of living organisms, such as providing for orderly energy transformations, maintaining homeostatis, reproducing, and metabolism and growth. Organ systems must perform a variety of processes common to all living organisms (a listing of these processes can be found above, in Skill 11.1). Skill 12.1 discusses several major systems of plants, and Skill 12.2 surveys the major organ systems of animals.

COMPETENCY 012   UNDERSTAND THE STRUCTURES AND FUNCTIONS OF SYSTEMS IN PLANTS AND ANIMALS

Skill 12.1   Demonstrating knowledge of the relationship between structure and function in the major systems in plants

Roots, stems, leaves, and reproductive structures are the most functionally important parts of plant anatomy. Different types of plants have distinctive anatomical structures. Thus, a discussion of plant anatomy requires an understanding of the classifications of plants.

PLANT ANATOMY

Roots

Roots absorb water and minerals and exchange gases in the soil. Like stems, roots contain xylem and phloem. Xylem transports water and minerals, called xylem sap, upward. The sugar produced by photosynthesis goes down the phloem in phloem sap, traveling to the roots and other non-photosynthetic parts of the plant. In addition to water and mineral absorption, roots anchor plants in place, preventing erosion by environmental conditions.

Stems

Stems are the major support structure of plants. Stems consist primarily of three types of tissue: dermal, ground, and vascular. **Dermal tissue** covers the outside surface of the stem to prevent excessive water loss and control gas exchange. **Ground tissue** consists mainly of parenchyma cells and surrounds the vascular tissue, providing support and protection. Finally, **vascular tissue**, xylem and phloem, provides long-distance transport of nutrients and water.

Leaves

Leaves enable plants to capture light and carbon dioxide for photosynthesis. Photosynthesis occurs primarily in the leaves. Plants exchange gases through their leaves via stomata, small openings on the underside of the leaves. Stomata allow oxygen to move in or out of the plant and carbon dioxide to move in. Leaf size and shape varies greatly between species of plants and botanists often identify plants by their characteristic leaf patterns.

Reproductive Structures

The sporophyte (diploid) generation is the dominant phase in plant reproduction and makes up almost their entire life cycle. Sporophytes contain a diploid set of chromosomes and form haploid spores by meiosis. Spores develop into gametophytes (the haploid generation) that produce male or female gametes by mitosis. Finally, the male and female gametes fuse, producing a diploid zygote that develops into a new sporophyte.

Angiosperm reproductive structures are the flowers.

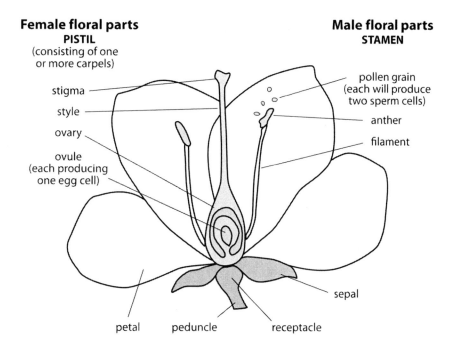

The male gametophytes are pollen grains and the female gametophytes are embryo sacs that are inside the ovules. The male pollen grains form in the anthers at the tips of the stamens. The ovaries contain the female ovules. Finally, the stamen is the reproductive organ of the male and the carpel is the reproductive organ of the female.

Skill 12.2   Demonstrating knowledge of the relationship between structure and function in the major systems in animals

In the following paragraphs, several major organ systems are described. Note how the structure of each system component matches the function of that component.

DIGESTION

The function of the digestive system is to break food down into nutrients and absorb it into the blood stream, where it can be delivered to all cells of the body for use in cellular respiration.

Nutrients

Essential nutrients are those nutrients that the body needs but cannot make. There are four groups of essential nutrients: essential amino acids, essential fatty acids, vitamins, and minerals.

There are ten essential amino acids humans need. A lack of these amino acids results in protein deficiency. There are only a few essential fatty acids.

Vitamins are organic molecules essential for a nutritionally adequate diet. Nutritionists have identified thirteen vitamins essential to humans.

There are two groups of vitamins: water-soluble (includes vitamin B complex and vitamin C) and water insoluble (vitamins A, D and K). Vitamin deficiencies can cause severe problems.

Unlike vitamins, minerals are inorganic molecules. Calcium is needed for bone construction and maintenance. Iron is important in cellular respiration and is a major component of hemoglobin.

Carbohydrates, fats, and proteins fuel the generation of ATP. Water is necessary to keep the body hydrated.

Components of the Human Digestive System

The teeth and saliva begin digestion by breaking down food into smaller pieces and lubricating it so it can be swallowed. The lips, cheeks, and tongue form a bolus, or ball of food. It is carried down the pharynx by the process of peristalsis (wave-like contractions) and enters the stomach through the sphincter, which closes to keep food from going back up. In the stomach, pepsinogen and hydrochloric acid form pepsin, the enzyme that hydrolyzes proteins. Pepsin and other chemicals break down the food further and it is churned into acid chyme. The pyloric sphincter muscle opens to allow food to enter the small intestine.

Most nutrient absorption occurs in the small intestine. Its large surface area, a function of its length and protrusions called villi and microvilli, provides the primary absorptive surface into the bloodstream. After leaving the stomach, acidic chyme is neutralized in the small intestine to allow the enzymes necessary to break down food to function. Accessory organs, such as the pancreas and liver, produce these enzymes and bile. The liver makes bile, which breaks down and emulsifies fatty acids.

Any remaining food then enters the large intestine. The large intestine functions to reabsorb water and produce vitamin K. The feces, or remaining waste, passes out through the anus.

Disorders of the Digestive System

Gastric ulcers are lesions in the stomach lining. Ulcers are mainly caused by bacteria, but are worsened by pepsin and acid.

Appendicitis refers to inflammation of the appendix. The appendix has no known function, is open to the intestine, and can be blocked by hardened stool or swollen tissue. A blocked appendix can cause bacterial infections and inflammation, leading to appendicitis. If left untreated, the appendix can rupture, allowing stool and infection to spill out into the abdomen. Without immediate surgery this condition can be life-threatening. Symptoms of appendicitis include lower abdominal pain, nausea, loss of appetite, and fever.

CIRCULATION

The function of the closed circulatory system (**cardiovascular system**) is to carry oxygenated blood and nutrients to all cells of the body and return carbon dioxide waste to the lungs for expulsion.

Components of the Human Circulatory (Cardiovascular) System

The heart, blood vessels, and blood make up the cardiovascular system.

The heart

The structure of the heart is shown below:

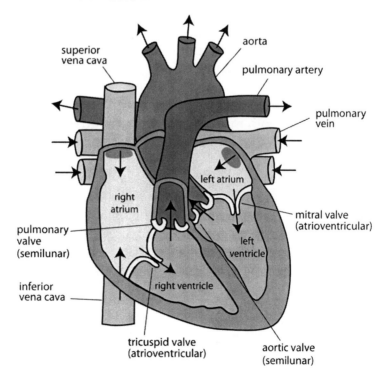

The **atria** are the chambers that receive blood returning to the heart, and the **ventricles** are the chambers that pump blood out of the heart. There are four valves in the heart: two atrioventricular (AV) valves and two semilunar valves. The AV valves are located between each atrium and ventricle. The contraction of the ventricles closes the AV valve to keep blood from flowing back into the atria. The semilunar valves are located where the aorta leaves the left ventricle and where the pulmonary artery leaves the right ventricle. The semilunar valves are opened by ventricular contraction, allowing blood to be pumped out into the arteries, and are closed by ventricular relaxation.

Cardiac output is the volume of blood per minute that the left ventricle pumps. This output depends on heart rate and stroke volume. **Heart rate** is the number of times the heart beats per minute and **stroke volume** is the amount of blood pumped by the left ventricle per contraction. Humans have an average cardiac output of about 5.25 L/min. Heavy exercise can increase cardiac output up to five times. Epinephrine and increased body temperature also increase heart rate and cardiac output.

Cardiac muscle can contract without any signal from the nervous system. The sinoatrial node is the pacemaker of the heart. The sinoatrial node is located on the wall of the right atrium and generates electrical impulses that make cardiac muscle cells contract in unison. The atrioventricular node shortly delays the electrical impulse to ensure that the atria empty before the ventricles contract.

Blood vessels

There are three kinds of blood vessels in the circulatory system: arteries, capillaries, and veins. **Arteries** carry oxygenated blood away from the heart to organs in the body. Arteries branch off to form smaller arterioles in organs. Arterioles form tiny **capillaries** that reach every tissue. Downstream, capillaries combine to form larger venules. Venules combine to form larger **veins** that return blood to the heart. Arteries and veins differ in the direction in which they carry blood.

Blood vessels are lined by endothelium. In veins and arteries, the endothelium is surrounded by a layer of smooth muscle and an outer layer of elastic connective tissue. Capillaries consist only of the thin endothelium layer and its basement membrane that allows for nutrient absorption.

Blood flow velocity decreases as it reaches the capillaries. The capillaries have the smallest diameter of all the blood vessels, but this is not why the velocity decreases. Arteries carry blood to such a large number of capillaries that the blood flow velocity actually decelerates as it enters the capillaries. **Blood pressure** is the hydrostatic force that blood exerts against the wall of a vessel. Blood pressure is greatest in arteries.

Blood

Blood is a connective tissue consisting of liquid plasma and several kinds of cells. Approximately 60% of blood is plasma. Plasma contains water salts called electrolytes, as well as nutrients, waste, and proteins. The electrolytes maintain a pH of about 7.4. The proteins contribute to blood viscosity and help maintain pH. Some of the proteins include clotting factors and immunoglobulins, the antibodies that help fend off infection.

The lymphatic system is responsible for returning lost fluid and proteins to the blood. Fluid enters lymph capillaries. This lymph fluid is filtered by lymph nodes that are filled with white blood cells to fight infection.

Types of blood cells

There are two classes of cells in blood: red blood cells and white blood cells. **Red blood cells (erythrocytes)** are the most numerous. They contain hemoglobin, which carries oxygen.

White blood cells (leukocytes) are larger than red blood cells. They are phagocytic and have the ability to engulf invaders. White blood cells are not confined to the blood vessels and can enter the interstitial fluid between cells. There are five types of white blood cells: monocytes, neutrophils, basophils, eosinophils, and lymphocytes.

A third cellular element found in blood is platelets. **Platelets** are made in the bone marrow and assist in blood clotting. The neurotransmitter that initiates blood vessel constriction following an injury is called serotonin. A material called prothrombin is converted to thrombin with the help of thrombokinase. The thrombin is then used to convert fibrinogen to fibrin, which traps red blood cells to form a scab and stop blood flow.

Diseases of the Circulatory (Cardiovascular) System

Cardiovascular diseases are the leading cause of death in the United States. Cardiac disease usually manifests as either a heart attack or stroke. During a heart attack, cardiac muscle tissue dies, usually from coronary artery blockage. During a stroke, nervous tissue in the brain dies due to the blockage of arteries in the head.

Many heart attacks and strokes are caused by a disease called **atherosclerosis**. Plaques form on the inner walls of arteries, narrowing the area through which blood can flow. Arteriosclerosis is when the arteries harden from plaque accumulation. Atherosclerosis can be prevented by a healthy diet that limits lipids and cholesterol, and regular exercise. High blood pressure (hypertension) promotes atherosclerosis. Diet, medication, and exercise can reduce high blood pressure and prevent atherosclerosis.

RESPIRATION

Animals constantly require oxygen for cellular respiration and need to remove carbon dioxide from their bodies. The respiratory surface must be large and moist. Different animal groups have different types of respiratory organs that perform gas exchange.

Methods of Respiration

Some animals, like worms, use their entire outer skin for respiration.

Fish and other aquatic animals have gills for gas exchange. Ventilation increases the flow of water over the gills. This process brings in oxygen and removes carbon dioxide through the gills. Fish use a large amount of energy to ventilate their gills. This is because the oxygen available in water is less than that available in the air.

Arthropoda (insects) have tracheal tubes that send air to all parts of their bodies. Gas exchange for smaller insects is provided by diffusion. Larger insects ventilate their bodies using a series of body movements that compress and expand the tracheal tubes. All vertebrates, including humans, have lungs as their primary respiratory organ.

Components of the Human Respiratory System

As the primary respiratory organ of the human respiratory system, the lungs contain a dense network of capillaries just beneath the epithelium. The surface area of the epithelium is about 100 m^2 in humans. Based on the surface area, the volume of air inhaled and exhaled is the tidal volume. This is normally about 500 mL in adults. Vital capacity is the maximum volume the lungs can inhale and exhale. This is usually around 3400 mL.

The Respiratory Process

The respiratory system functions in the gas exchange of oxygen and carbon dioxide waste. It delivers oxygen to the bloodstream and picks up carbon dioxide for release out of the body. Air enters the mouth and nose, where it is warmed, moistened, and filtered of dust and particles. Cilia in the trachea trap unwanted material in mucus, which can be expelled. The trachea splits into two bronchial tubes, which divide into smaller and smaller bronchioles in the lungs.

The internal surface of the lung is composed of alveoli, which are thin-walled air sacs. These allow for a large surface area for gas exchange. The alveoli are lined with capillaries. Oxygen diffuses into the bloodstream and carbon dioxide diffuses out of the capillaries to be exhaled out of the lungs. The oxygenated blood is carried to the heart and delivered to all parts of the body by hemoglobin, a protein consisting of iron.

The thoracic cavity holds the lungs. The diaphragm muscle below the lungs is an adaptation that makes inhalation possible. As the volume of the thoracic cavity increases, the diaphragm muscle flattens out, and inhalation occurs.

Diseases of the Respiratory System

Emphysema is a chronic obstructive pulmonary disease (COPD). Pulmonary diseases make it difficult for a person to breathe. Airflow through the bronchial tubes is partially blocked, making breathing difficult. The primary cause of emphysema is cigarette smoke. People with a deficiency in alpha$_1$-antitrypsin protein production have a greater risk of developing emphysema at an earlier age. This protein helps protect the lungs from inflammatory damage. This deficiency is rare, and can be tested for in individuals with a family history of the disease. There is no cure for emphysema, but there are treatments available. The best way to prevent emphysema is to avoid smoking.

EXCRETION

Methods of Excretion

In many invertebrates, osmoregulation and excretion involves tubular systems. The tubules branch throughout the body. Interstitial fluid enters these tubes and is collected into excretory ducts that empty into the external environment through openings in the body wall. Insects have excretory organs called Malpighian tubes. These organs pump water, salts, and nitrogenous waste into the tubules. These fluids then pass through the hindgut and out the rectum.

Components of the Human Excretory System

Vertebrates have kidneys as the primary excretion organ. Each kidney in the adult human is about 10 cm long. They receive about 20% of the blood pumped with each heartbeat, despite their small size. The function of the excretory system is to rid the body of nitrogenous wastes in the form of urea.

The smallest functional unit of excretion in the kidney is the nephron. The structures of the kidney and the nephron are shown below:

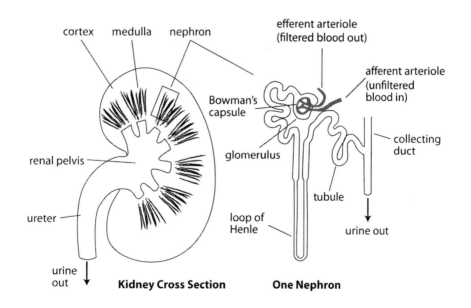

Kidney Cross Section   One Nephron

The Bowman's capsule contains the glomerulus, a tightly packed group of capillaries in the nephron. The glomerulus is under high pressure. Water, urea, salts, and other fluids leak out due to pressure into the Bowman's capsule. This fluid waste (filtrate) passes through the three regions of the nephron: the proximal convoluted tubule, the loop of Henle, and the distal tubule. In the proximal convoluted tubule, unwanted molecules are secreted into the filtrate. In the loop of Henle, salt is actively pumped out of the tube and much water is lost due to the hyperosmosity of the inner part (medulla) of the kidney. As the fluid enters the distal tubule, more water is reabsorbed.

Urine forms in the collecting duct that leads to the ureter, then to the bladder, where it is stored. Urine is passed from the bladder through the urethra. The amount of water reabsorbed back into the body is dependent upon how much water or fluids an individual has consumed. Urine can be very dilute or very concentrated depending on fluid consumption.

Disorders of the Excretory System

Glomerulonephritis (GN), often more generally called nephritis, usually occurs in children. Symptoms include hypertension, decreased renal function, hematuria, and edema. Nephritis is produced by an antigen-antibody complex that causes inflammation and cell proliferation. Nephritis causes normal kidney tissue to become damaged and, if left untreated, can lead to kidney failure and death.

NERVOUS CONTROL

Components of the Human Nervous System

The **central nervous system (CNS)** consists of the brain and spinal cord. The CNS is responsible for the body's response to environmental stimuli. The spinal cord sends out motor commands that are automated or reflexive in response to stimuli. The brain is where responses to more complex stimuli occur. The meninges are the connective tissues that protect the CNS. The CNS contains fluid-filled spaces called ventricles. These ventricles are filled with cerebrospinal fluid, which is formed in the brain. Cerebrospinal fluid cushions the brain and circulates nutrients, white blood cells, and hormones.

The **peripheral nervous system (PNS)** consists of the nerves that connect the CNS to the rest of the body. The sensory division brings information to the CNS from sensory receptors, and the motor division sends signals from the CNS to effector cells.

The motor division consists of the somatic nervous system and the autonomic nervous system. The somatic nervous system is controlled consciously in response to external stimuli. The autonomic nervous system is unconsciously controlled by the hypothalamus of the brain, thereby regulating the body's internal environment. This system is responsible for the movement of smooth and cardiac muscles as well as the muscles for other organ systems.

The **neuron** is the basic unit of the nervous system. It consists of an axon, which carries impulses away from the cell body; the dendrite, which carries impulses toward the cell body; and the cell body, which contains the nucleus. The myelin sheath, comprised of Schwann cells, covers the neuron and provides insulation, which allows electrical impulses to travel quickly through the neuron. **Synapses** are junction between neurons. Chemicals called **neurotransmitters** serve as signaling molecules that are released from one neuron and diffuse through the synaptic cleft to another neuron.

Nerve action depends on an imbalance of electrical charges between the inside and outside of the neuron. These electrical charges are carried by ions such as sodium, calcium, and potassium. When the ions move from one side of the neuronal membrane to the other (from outside the cell to inside it, or vice versa), an electrical current flows through the neuron. These electrical currents are called action potentials. Action potentials trigger the release of neurotransmitters from the axon into the synaptic cleft. When the neurotransmitters diffuse through the synaptic cleft, they bind to receptors on the surface of dendrites. This binding then triggers another action potential in the next neuron.

When a neuron is resting, it has a negative charge and is said to be hyperpolarized. When ions like sodium flow into the neuron, it takes on a positive charge, becoming depolarized, and an action potential is generated.

Some neurons, or nerves, synapse on muscle cells. This is called a neuromuscular junction. In neuromuscular junctions, there is a threshold of neurotransmitters that must be released by the nerve in order to generate a response from the muscle cell. This is called an "all or none" response.

Nervous System Disorders

There are many nervous system disorders. Parkinson's disease is caused by the degeneration of the basal ganglia, the brain region that controls motor movement. This causes a breakdown in the transmission of motor impulses to the muscles. Symptoms include tremors, slow movement, and muscle rigidity. Progression of Parkinson's disease occurs in five stages: early, mild, moderate, advanced, and severe. In the severe stage, an afflicted person is confined to a bed or chair. There is no cure for Parkinson's disease. Private research with stem cells is currently underway to find a cure for Parkinson's disease.

CONTRACTILE SYSTEMS AND MOVEMENT

Components of the Human Muscular System

The function of the muscular system is to facilitate movement. There are three types of muscle tissue: skeletal, cardiac, and smooth.

1. **Skeletal muscle** is voluntary. These muscles are attached to bones and are responsible for their movement. Skeletal muscle consists of long fibers and is striated due to the repeating patterns of myofilaments (made of the proteins actin and myosin) that make up the fibers.
2. **Cardiac muscle** is found in the heart. Cardiac muscle is striated like skeletal muscle, but differs in that the plasma membrane of the cardiac muscle causes the muscle to beat even when it is away from the heart. The action potentials of cardiac and skeletal muscles also differ.
3. **Smooth muscle** is involuntary. It is found in organs and enables functions such as digestion and respiration. Unlike skeletal and cardiac muscle, smooth muscle is not striated. Smooth muscle has less myosin and does not generate as much tension as the striated muscles.

The mechanism of skeletal muscle contraction involves a nerve impulse striking a muscle fiber. This causes calcium ions to flood the sarcomere. The myosin fibers creep along the actin, causing the muscle to contract. Once the nerve impulse has passed, calcium is pumped out and the contraction ends.

Components of the Human Skeletal System

The **axial skeleton** consists of the skull and vertebral bones. The **appendicular skeleton** consists of the shoulder girdle, arms, legs, and tailbones. Bone is a connective tissue. Parts of the bone include:

1. Compact bone, which provides strength
2. Spongy bone, which contains red marrow to make blood cells
3. Yellow marrow in the center of long bones, which stores fat cells
4. The periosteum, which is the protective covering on the outside of the bone

Joints

In addition to bones and muscles, ligaments and tendons are important joint components. A joint is a place where two bones meet. Joints enable movement. Ligaments attach bone to bone, and tendons attach bone to muscle. There are three types of joints:

1. Ball and socket: Allows for rotational movement. There is a ball and socket joint between the shoulder and humerus. This type of joint allows the arms and legs to move in many different directions.
2. Hinge: Movement is restricted to a single plane. An example of a hinge joint is between the humerus and ulna.
3. Pivot: Allows for the rotation of the forearm at the elbow and the hands at the wrist.

Types of Support Systems

The support system provides structure for the body. There are various kinds of support systems in animals.

- Lower invertebrates do not have a support system as such. Their bodies are made up of muscles, and they either crawl or drag themselves about.
- Soft-bodied animals do not have a support structure, but almost all (excluding slugs) have shells. These shells offer protection from predators.
- Complex invertebrates have exoskeletons, which are located outside the body. Exoskeletons are made up of a number of hardened plates, which support the animal, give it shape, and protect it from predators.
- Vertebrates have a support structure made up of a number of bead-like structures known as vertebrae. Vertebrates also have an endoskeleton. An endoskeleton is a skeleton that is present inside the body. While exoskeletons limit the growth of the body, endoskeletons do not.
- A **chordate** is an animal that, at some time in its life, has a tough, flexible rod that runs along its back. Vertebrates are chordates. In most vertebrates, the rod along the back is replaced by a backbone.

INTEGUMENTARY SYSTEM (THE SKIN)

The skin consists of two distinct layers. The **epidermis** is the thin outer layer and the **dermis** is the thick inner layer. Layers of tightly packed epithelial cells make up the epidermis. The tight packaging of the epithelial cells supports the skin's function as a protective barrier against outside elements.

The top layer of the epidermis consists of dead skin cells and is filled with keratin, a waterproofing protein. The dermis consists of connective tissue. It contains blood vessels, hair follicles, sweat glands, and sebaceous glands. An oily secretion called sebum, produced by the sebaceous glands, is released to the outer epidermis through the hair follicles. Sebum maintains the pH of the skin between 3 and 5, which inhibits most microbial growth.

The skin also plays a role in thermoregulation. Increased body temperature causes skin blood vessels to dilate, resulting in the loss of heat from the skin's surface. Sweat glands are also activated, increasing evaporative cooling. Decreased body temperature causes skin blood vessels to constrict. This results in the diversion of blood from the skin to deeper tissues, thereby reducing heat loss from the surface of the skin.

Skill 12.3 Predicting the system function of a given structure based on its characteristics and components

Having seen that structure aligns with function (see Skill 12.2) one can generally guess at the function of a structure based on its characteristics and components. For example, when dissecting an organism structure consisting of bounded tubes and muscular pumps, one could guess that the structure probably is part of the organism's circulatory system. Of course, these types of assumptions must be borne out through scientific investigation before they are demonstrated to be correct.

COMPETENCY 013   **UNDERSTAND THE HUMAN IMMUNE SYSTEM, HUMAN DISEASES, AND PRINCIPLES OF DISEASE PREVENTION**

Skill 13.1   Recognizing components of the human immune system and their functions

The immune system is responsible for defending the body against foreign invaders. There are two types of defense mechanisms: non-specific and specific.

THE NON-SPECIFIC IMMUNE MECHANISM

The **non-specific** immune mechanism is comprised of two parts. The body's physical barriers are the first line of defense. These include the skin and mucous membranes. The skin prevents the penetration of bacteria and viruses as long as there are no abrasions on the skin. Mucous membranes form a protective barrier around the digestive, respiratory, and genitourinary tracts. In addition, the pH of the skin and mucous membranes inhibit the growth of many microbes. Mucous secretions (tears and saliva) wash away many microbes, and also contain lysozymes that kill many microbes.

The second component of the non-specific immune response includes white blood cells and inflammatory responses. **Phagocytosis** is the process of engulfing foreign particles with the cell membrane to form an internal phagosome. Neutrophils make up about seventy percent of all white blood cells. Monocytes mature to become macrophages, which are the largest phagocytic cells.

Eosinophils are also phagocytic. Natural killer cells destroy the body's own infected cells instead of directly destroying the invading microbe. During an inflammatory response, blood supply to the injured area is increased, causing redness and heat. Swelling also typically occurs with inflammation. Histamine is released by basophils and mast cells when cells are injured, triggering the inflammatory response.

THE SPECIFIC IMMUNE MECHANISM

The **specific** immune mechanism recognizes specific foreign material and responds by destroying the invader. These mechanisms are specific and diverse. They are able to recognize individual pathogens. An **antigen** is any foreign particle that elicits an immune response. An **antibody** is manufactured by the body to specifically recognize and latch onto antigens to destroy them. Memory of the invaders provides immunity upon further exposure.

Skill 13.2 Demonstrating knowledge of immune system responses that take place in cells, tissues, organs, and organ systems throughout the progression of a given viral, bacterial, fungal, or parasitic disease

Immunity is the body's ability to recognize and destroy an antigen before it causes harm. Active immunity develops after recovery from an infectious disease (e.g., chickenpox) or after a vaccination (e.g., mumps, measles, and rubella). Passive immunity can be passed from one individual to another and is not permanent. A good example of passive immunity the immunity passed from mother to nursing child. A baby's immune system is not well-developed, and the passive immunity babies receive through nursing provides them with additional protection.

There are two main responses made by the body after exposure to an antigen: humoral and cell-mediated.

1. **Humoral response**: Free antigens and antigen-presenting cells activate B cells (lymphocytes from bone marrow), which transform into plasma cells that secrete antibodies. Memory cells that recognize future exposure to the same antigen are also generated. Antibodies defend the body against extracellular pathogens by binding to the antigens and making them an easy target for phagocytes to engulf and destroy. Antibodies are in a class of proteins called immunoglobulins. There are five major classes of immunoglobulins (Ig) involved in the humoral response: IgM, IgG, IgA, IgD, and IgE.

2. **Cell-mediated response**: Infected cells activate T cells (lymphocytes from the thymus), which then bind to the infected cells and destroy them along with the antigen. T cell receptors on T helper cells recognize antigens bound to the body's own cells. T helper cells release IL-2, which stimulates other lymphocytes (cytotoxic T cells and B cells). Cytotoxic T cells kill infected host cells by recognizing specific antigens.

Skill 13.3 Recognizing causes and characteristics of common human diseases (e.g., influenza, malaria, cancer), including risk factors

CAUSES OF HUMAN DISEASES

Infectious Agents

Many human diseases are caused by infectious agents. Bacteria cause many diseases, such as tuberculosis, that are significant causes of mortality and morbidity. Most bacterial diseases successfully can be treated by the use of antibiotic drugs.

Viruses

Viruses cause many diseases, such as influenza, that are significant causes of mortality and morbidity. AIDS is caused by a viral infection. Most viral diseases are difficult to treat with drug therapy, but advances in anti-viral drugs are rapid.

Protists

Protists cause some diseases, such as malaria. Malaria is one of the most widespread and serious diseases extant in the world today. Malarial treatment is complicated because the disease-causing pathogen is eukaryotic and exhibits a complex life cycle; most infected people live in regions where constant exposure and re-exposure are routine.

Cancer

Cancer is a broad class of diseases caused by cells in a living organism failing to respond to normal cell-cycle control stimuli. These cells grow out of control, consuming resources and damaging normal-functioning cells and tissues.

The cell cycle

The restriction point in the cell cycle occurs late in the G_1 phase of the cell cycle. This is when the decision for the cell to divide is made. If all the internal and external cell systems are working properly, the cell proceeds to replicate. Cells may also decide not to proceed past the restriction point. This nondividing cell state is called the G_0 phase. Many specialized cells remain in this state.

The density of cells also regulates cell division. Density-dependent inhibition occurs when cells crowd one another and consume all available nutrients, thereby halting cell division. Cancer cells do not respond to density-dependent inhibition. They divide excessively and invade other tissues. As long as there are nutrients, cancer cells are "immortal."

DISEASE PREVENTION

Many diseases have well-documented risk factors that can notably reduce the likelihood of experiencing the disease. Good personal hygiene, access to clean drinking water and sterile food sources, and safe-sex practices all foster a decrease in disease. Safe-sex practices have been successful in reducing sexually transmitted diseases. Smoking cessation notably reduces the risk of certain prevalent types of cancer. Diets high in fiber and low in some types of fat have also been linked to lower risk factors for some types of cancer.

Skill 13.4   Applying knowledge of methods for preventing or treating common human diseases

Vaccines are antigens given in very small amounts. They stimulate both humoral and cell-mediated responses and help memory cells recognize future exposure to the antigen so antibodies can be produced much more quickly. The immune system attacks not only microbes, but also cells that are not native to the host, such as skin grafts, organ transplantations, and blood transfusions. Antibodies to foreign blood and tissue types already exist in the body. If blood is transfused that is not compatible with the host, these antibodies destroy the new blood cells. There is a similar reaction when tissue and organs are transplanted.

The major histocompatibility complex (MHC) is responsible for the rejection of tissue and organ transplants. This complex is unique to each person. Cytotoxic T cells recognize the MHC on transplanted tissue or organ as foreign and destroy these tissues. Various drugs are needed to suppress the immune system and prevent rejection of foreign tissue; however, this also leaves the patient more susceptible to infection.

Autoimmune disease occurs when the body's own immune system destroys its own cells. Lupus, Grave's disease, and rheumatoid arthritis are examples of autoimmune diseases. There is no way to prevent autoimmune diseases. Immunodeficiency is a deficiency in either the humoral or cell-mediated immune defenses. HIV is an example of an immunodeficiency disease.

DOMAIN V   DIVERSITY AND BIOLOGICAL EVOLUTION

COMPETENCY 014   UNDERSTAND THE DEVELOPMENT OF ADAPTATIONS
                                     IN RESPONSE TO ENVIRONMENTAL STRESSES

Skill 14.1   **Recognizing the relationship between conditions in an organism's environment and the development of adaptations**

Adaptations are phenotypic traits that allow an organism to be more competitive within its environment. Classical evolution theorizes that the accumulation of adaptations leads to fit individuals, populations, and species. Given this theory, we would expect to find that nearly all living things are quite well adapted to their environments. As an environment changes, we would expect to see gradual innovation in novel adaptations to allow organisms to more fully exploit the changing environment. Species unable to functionally adapt to a constantly changing environment can face extinction.

For example, plants require adaptations that allow them to absorb light for photosynthesis. Because they are unable to move about, they must evolve methods to allow them to reproduce successfully. As time passed, plants moved from a water environment to the land. Advantages of life on land included more available light and a higher concentration of carbon dioxide. Originally, there were no predators and less competition for space on land. Plants had to evolve methods of support, reproduction, respiration, and conservation of water once they moved to land.

Plant reproduction occurs through an alternation of generations, meaning that a haploid stage in the plant's life history alternates with a diploid stage. Specific plant tissues evolved in order to obtain water and minerals from the earth. The plant's wax cuticle prevents the loss of water, while the leaves capture light and carbon dioxide for photosynthesis. Stomata provide openings on the underside of leaves for oxygen to move in or out of the plant and for carbon dioxide to move in. Roots evolved to provide a method of anchorage, and the polymer lignin evolved to provide structural support.

Skill 14.2   **Demonstrating knowledge of the range of physical, behavioral, and biochemical adaptations that can occur in response to environmental stresses**

All adaptations arise in response to natural selection and thus can be understood as occurring in response to environmental stresses. Adaptations need not be the best possible solution to a problem—indeed, they seldom are—but instead represent a tradeoff and are best understood from a cost-benefit analysis perspective.

Adaptations can be at the physical, behavioral, or biochemical level. Physical adaptations are things like eyes, wings, teeth, and fur. Behavioral adaptations are generally constrained by an organism's ability to exhibit plastic behaviors. Biochemical adaptations include immune response, energy utilization, and some systems of interspecies gamete recognition. For example, plants demonstrate a wide range of adaptations, as discussed in the following paragraphs.

ADAPTATION AND EVOLUTION IN PLANTS

Non-vascular Plants

The **non-vascular plants** represent an evolutionary grade characterized by several primitive features: lack of roots, lack of conducting tissues, reliance on absorption of water that falls on the plant or condenses on the plant in high humidity, and a lack of leaves. Non-vascular plants include the liverworts, hornworts, and mosses. Each of these is recognized as a separate division.

Vascular Plants

The characteristics of **vascular plants** are as follows: they contain lignin, which provides rigidity and strength to cell walls for upright growth, tracheid cells for water transport, sieve cells for nutrient transport, and underground stems (rhizomes) as a structure from which adventitious roots originate.

There are two kinds of vascular plants: non-seeded and seeded. The non-seeded vascular plant divisions include Division Lycophyta (club mosses), Division Sphenophyta (horsetails), and Division Pterophyta (ferns). The seeded vascular plants differ from the non-seeded plants in their method of reproduction, which we will discuss later. Vascular seed plants are divided into two groups, the gymnosperms and the angiosperms.

Seeded vascular plants

Gymnosperms were the first plants to use of seeds for reproduction, which made them less dependent on water to assist in reproduction. Their seeds and the pollen from the male are carried by the wind. Gymnosperms have cones that protect the seeds. Gymnosperm divisions include Division Cycadophyta (cycads), Division Ginkgophyta (ginkgo), Division Gnetophyta (gnetophytes), and Division Coniferophyta (conifers).

Angiosperms are the largest group in the plant kingdom. They are the flowering plants and produce true seeds for reproduction. Angiosperms arose about seventy million years ago, when dinosaurs were disappearing. The land was drying up and the plants' ability to produce seeds that could remain dormant until conditions became acceptable allowed for their success.

Angiosperms also have more advanced vascular tissue and larger leaves for increased photosynthesis. Angiosperms consist of only one division, the Anthrophyta. Angiosperms are divided into monocots and dicots. Monocots have one cotelydon (seed leaf) and parallel veins on their leaves. Their flower petals are in multiples of threes.

Dicots have two cotelydons and branching veins on their leaves. Their flower petals are in multiples of fours or fives.

Skill 14.3   Applying knowledge of biological principles to explain how a specific adaptation of a given species may have developed

The process of adaptation development is simply the process of natural or sexual selection acting on heritable variation within a population to select for traits that are most fit to the environment.

For example, suppose a given snail population exists in a particular environment where the snails are heavily preyed upon by birds. Snail shell coloration is variable and snails with darker-colored shells are more difficult to see than those with lighter shells. Snail shell thickness is variable, and thicker-shelled snails are more difficult to eat. Over time we would expect to see the snail population develop thicker and darker shells. Alternately, behavioral adaptations might arise that allow snails to evade predators. Alternately, biochemical adaptations might arise that make snails unpalatable or poisonous.

For any of these adaptations to arise, there must first be genetic variability that is acted upon by natural or sexual selection. For example, if no genetic variability in snail toxicity exists, then we would not expect to see a poisonous snail species evolve. Natural and sexual selection do not create novel features—they simply refine the genetic variability produced by mutation and recombination.

COMPETENCY 015 **UNDERSTAND THE SIGNIFICANCE OF GENETIC VARIATION WITHIN A POPULATION AND FACTORS THAT INFLUENCE THE RANGE OF PHENOTYPES IN A POPULATION OF A SPECIES**

Skill 15.1 **Recognizing sources of genetic variation within a population and ways of representing (e.g., diagrams, statistical relationships) the range of phenotypes in a population in a given environment**

Heritable variation is responsible for the individuality of organisms. An individual's phenotype is based on an inherited genotype and the surrounding environment. Mutation and sexual recombination creates genetic variation. **Mutations** can be errors in replication or spontaneous rearrangements of one or more segments of DNA.

Mutations contribute a minimal amount of variation to a population. It is the unique **recombination** of existing alleles that cause the majority of genetic differences. Recombination is caused by the crossing over of the parent genes during meiosis. This results in unique offspring. With all the possible mating combinations in the world, it is obvious how sexual reproduction is the primary cause of genetic variation.

Natural selection is based on the survival of certain traits in a population over the course of time. The phrase "survival of the fittest" is often associated with natural selection. Fitness is the contribution an individual makes to the gene pool of the next generation.

Natural selection acts on phenotypes. An organism's phenotype is constantly exposed to its environment. Based on an organism's phenotype, selection indirectly adapts a population to its environment by maintaining favorable genotypes in the gene pool.

Skill 15.2 **Demonstrating knowledge of factors that can change the frequency of alleles and genotypes in a population (e.g., nonrandom mating, genetic drift, natural selection)**

Evolution is currently defined as a change in genotype over time. Gene frequencies shift and change from generation to generation. Populations evolve, not individuals.

THE HARDY-WEINBERG THEORY OF GENE EQUILIBRIUM

The **Hardy-Weinberg theory** of gene equilibrium is a mathematical prediction to show shifting gene patterns. Let us use the letter "*A*" to represent the dominant condition of normal skin pigment, and the letter "*a*" to represent the recessive condition of albinism. In a population, there are three possible genotypes: *AA, Aa* and *aa. AA* and *Aa* would have normal skin pigment, and only *aa* would be albinos.

According to the Hardy-Weinberg law, there are five requirements that keep gene frequency stable and limit evolution:

1. There is no mutation in the population.
2. There are no selection pressures; one gene is not more desirable in the environment.
3. There is no mating preference; mating is random.
4. The population is isolated; there is no immigration or emigration.
5. The population is large (mathematical probability is more accurate with a large sample).

The above conditions are extremely difficult to meet. If these five conditions are not met, then gene frequency can shift, leading to evolution. Let us say that 75% of a population has normal skin pigment (*AA* and *Aa*) and 25% are albino (*aa*). Using the following formula, we can determine the frequency of the *A* allele and the *a* allele in the population.

The formula is: $1 = p^2 + 2pq + q^2$; where 1 is the total population, p^2 is the number of *AA* individuals, $2pq$ is the number of *Aa* individuals, and q^2 is the number of *aa* individuals. This formula can be used over generations to determine if evolution is occurring.

Because you cannot tell by looking if an individual is *AA* or *Aa*, you must use the *aa* individuals to find that frequency first. As stated above, *aa* is 25% of the population. Because $aa = q^2$, we can determine the value of *q* (or *a*) by finding the square root of 0.25, which is 0.5. Therefore, 0.5 of the population has the *a* gene. In order to find the value for *p*, use the following formula: $1 = p + q$. This would make the value of *p* 0.5.

The **gene pool** is all the alleles at all gene loci in all individuals of a population. The Hardy-Weinberg theorem describes the gene pool in a non-evolving population. It states that the frequencies of alleles and genotypes in a population's gene pool are random unless acted on by something other than sexual recombination.

Now, to find the number of *AA*, plug it into the first formula:

- $AA = p^2 = 0.5 \times 0.5 = 0.25$
- $Aa = 2pq = 2(0.5 \times 0.5) = 0.5$
- $aa = q^2 = 0.5 \times 0.5 = 0.25$

Any question on the test dealing with the Hardy-Weinberg theorem will have an obvious squared number. The square of that number will be the frequency of the recessive gene, and you can figure anything else out knowing the formula and the frequency of *q*.

When frequencies vary from the Hardy-Weinberg equilibrium, the population is evolving. The change to the gene pool is on such a small scale that it is called microevolution.

Certain factors increase the chances of variability in a population, thus leading to evolution. Factors that increase variability include mutations, sexual reproduction, immigration, a large population, and variation in geographic locale. Factors that decrease variation are natural selection, emigration, a small population, and random mating.

Skill 15.3 Applying the principles of mutation, recombination, and natural selection to predict changes in the range of phenotypes in a species when a change occurs in the environment

Mutation (the ultimate source of all genetic variation), sexual and asexual recombination, and natural selection all lead to novel phenotypes within a given population. Some of these phenotypes are more fit in the current environmental paradigm. When the environmental paradigm changes, phenotypes that were less fit might become more fit. Because the environment is rarely completely stable over prolonged periods of time, a variety of novel phenotypes offers an avenue for natural selection to constantly refine or rework population genetics.

Also see Skill 15.2 for a discussion of the Hardy-Weinberg theorem, one simple mathematical model to explain shifting allele frequencies.

Skill 15.4 Demonstrating knowledge of how changes in the range of phenotypes within populations relate to evolution

Natural selection acts to reduce variability produced by mutation and recombination. If variability does not exist for a particular trait in a population, natural selection cannot select for or against novel implementations of the trait, and evolution cannot occur. For example, according to the Hardy-Weinberg theorem discussed in Skill 15.2, if we begin with the assumption that $p = 1$ and $q = 0$, it is clear that no amount of repetitive re-calculations will alter the allele frequency. In real-world species, however, variability is the rule.

Also see Skill 15.2.

COMPETENCY 016 **UNDERSTAND EVIDENCE OF EVOLUTIONARY RELATIONSHIPS BETWEEN SPECIES**

Skill 16.1 Demonstrating knowledge of significant features of the fossil record

Fossils are the key to understanding biological history. They are the preserved remnants left by an organism that lived in the past. Scientists have established the geological time scale to determine the age of a fossil. The geological time scale is broken down into four eras: Precambrian, Paleozoic, Mesozoic, and Cenozoic. The eras are further broken down into periods that represent distinct ages in the Earth's history.

Scientists use rock layers called **strata** to date fossils. The older layers of rock are at the bottom, which allows scientists to correlate rock layers with the era in which they were created. Radiometric dating is a more precise method of dating fossils. Rocks and fossils contain isotopes of elements accumulated over time. The isotope's half-life is used to date older fossils by determining the amount of isotope remaining and comparing it to the isotope's half-life.

Dating fossils is helpful in the construction of evolutionary trees. Scientists can arrange the succession of animals based on their fossil records. The fossils of an animal's ancestors can be dated and placed on its evolutionary tree. For example, the branched evolution of horses shows that the modern horse's ancestors were larger, had fewer toes, and had teeth modified for grazing.

Skill 16.2 Applying knowledge of biological principles to explain why some species are found in the fossil record relatively unchanged, while some species have changed and others have gone extinct

There are three modes of natural selection. **Stabilizing selection** favors the more common phenotypes, **directional selection** shifts the frequency of phenotypes in one direction, and **diversifying selection** favors individuals on both extremes of the phenotypic range.

Sexual selection leads to the secondary sex characteristics of males and females. Animals that use mating behaviors may be successful or unsuccessful. A male animal that lacks attractive plumage or has a weak mating call will not attract females, thereby eventually eliminating that gene from the gene pool. Mechanical isolation, where the male's sex organs do not fit the female, is an obvious disadvantage.

There are two theories about the rate of evolution. **Gradualism** is the theory that minor evolutionary changes occur at a regular rate. Darwin's book, *On the Origin of Species*, is based on the theory of gradualism.

Charles Darwin was born in 1809 and spent 5 years in his twenties on a ship called the *Beagle*. Of all the locations Darwin visited, he was most interested with the Galapagos Islands. There he collected 13 species of finches that were quite similar. He could not determine whether these finches were of the same species. He later learned these finches were, in fact, separate species. Darwin began to hypothesize that a new species arose from its ancestors by gradually collecting adaptations to a different environment. One of Darwin's best-known hypotheses involved the beak size of Galapagos finches. He theorized that the finches' beak sizes evolved to accommodate different food sources.

Although Darwin believed the origin of species was gradual, he was bewildered by gaps in the fossil records. **Punctuated equilibrium** is a model of evolution stating that species form rapidly over relatively short periods of geological history, and then progress through long periods of stasis with little or no change. Punctuationalists use fossil records to support their claim. It is probable that both gradualism and punctuated equilibrium both occur, depending on the particular lineage studied.

Skill 16.3   Applying knowledge of the evolutionary tree to explain and predict the morphological and genetic variations between two or more species

Convergent evolution is the development of similar biological structures in unrelated (or distantly related) species. The traits emerged not because the species share a recent common ancestor, but because the species were adapting to similar environmental factors or situations.

There are many examples of convergent evolution. Hedgehogs and porcupines both have prickly protrusions but are not close relatives. Squid and humans both have eyes. Silkworm moths, spiders, and weaver ants all produce silk threads. Koalas have fingerprints that are indinguishable from humans. And the classic example of convergent evolution is the wing. Birds and bats both have wings, but they are not closely related.

Skill 16.4   Analyzing fossil, morphological, genetic, and biochemical evidence and their use in determining evolutionary relationships between species

Comparative anatomy is the comparison of anatomical characteristics between or among different species. This includes the study of homologous and analogous structures. The comparison of DNA between or among species is the best way to establish evolutionary relationships. Organic chemistry is unrelated to evolutionary studies.

See also Skill 16.2 and Skill 16.3.

DOMAIN VI   INTERDEPENDENCE AND BEHAVIOR OF ORGANISMS

COMPETENCY 017   UNDERSTAND RELATIONSHIPS AMONG ORGANISMS AND BETWEEN ORGANISMS AND THEIR ENVIRONMENT

Skill 17.1   Demonstrating knowledge of the concepts of niche and habitat and of the basic requirements (e.g., nutrients, water, space) of organisms in their environment

The term "niche" describes the relational position of a species or population in an ecosystem. Niche includes how a population responds to the relative abundance of its resources and enemies (e.g., by growing when resources are abundant and predators, parasites, and pathogens are scarce). Niche also indicates the life history of an organism, habitat, and place in the food chain. According to the competitive exclusion principle, no two species can occupy the same niche in the same environment for a long time.

The full range of environmental conditions (biological and physical) under which an organism can exist describes its fundamental niche. When there is pressure from superior competitors, organisms are driven to occupy a narrower niche. This is known as the "realized niche."

Examples of niche:

Oak trees:

- live in forests
- absorb sunlight by photosynthesis
- provide shelter for many animals
- act as support for creeping plants
- serve as a source of food for animals
- cover the ground with dead leaves in the autumn

If the oak trees were cut down or destroyed by fire or storms they would no longer be doing their job, and this would have a disastrous effect on all the other organisms living in the same habitat.

Hedgehogs:

- eat a variety of insects and other invertebrates, which live underneath dead leaves and twigs
- have spines are a superb environment for fleas and ticks
- put nitrogen back into the soil when they urinate
- eat slugs, thereby protecting plants that the slugs would eat

If hedgehogs ceased to exist, the slug population would explode and the nutrients in the dead leaves and twigs would not be recycled.

Skill 17.2 **Demonstrating knowledge of the interrelationships and interdependence of organisms in a community (e.g., competition, mutualism, parasitism)**

All organisms must compete to survive. **Competition** generally focuses on access to resources such as habitat, food, and mates. Organisms often compete against other organisms of the same species, but often two distinct species compete within the same ecological niche. Individual organisms that cannot best others for these critical resources will die without reproducing. Several special types of inter-species interaction are possible between organisms. These include, but are not limited to, mutualism and parasitism.

Predation and **parasitism** are beneficial for one species and detrimental for the other. Predation is when a predator eats another species as prey. The common conception of predation is of a carnivore consuming other animals. This is one form of predation. Although it does not always result in the death of the plant, herbivory is also a form of predation. Some animals eat enough of a plant to cause the plant's death.

Parasitism involves a species that lives on or in another species, its host, causing detrimental effects to the host. Insects and viruses living off of and reproducing in their hosts are examples of parasitism.

Many plants and animals have evolved defenses against predators. Some plants have poisonous chemicals that will harm the predator if they are ingested, and some animals are camouflaged so they are more difficult for potential predators to detect.

Symbiosis is when two species live close together. Parasitism is one example of a symbiotic relationship. Another example of symbiosis is commensalism.

Commensalism occurs when one species benefits from the other without causing any harm to the other species. **Mutualism** is when both species benefit from one another. Species involved in mutualistic relationships must co-evolve to survive. As one species evolves, the other must evolve as well if it is to be successful. The grouper fish and a species of shrimp live in a mutualistic relationship. The shrimp feed off parasites that live on the grouper. Thus, the shrimp are fed and the grouper stays healthy. Many microorganisms exist in mutualistic relationships.

Skill 17.3   Demonstrating knowledge of methods for investigating and describing the relationships within and between species in an ecosystem and between organisms and their environment

Ecological descriptions of inter-species relationships are generally described as mutualism (both organisms benefit), commensalism (one organism benefits and one is unaffected), competition (both organisms are harmed), or parasitism (one organism benefits and one organism is harmed). When the relationship is particularly pervasive or close it often is called symbiosis.

See Skill 17.2 for a more-complete discussion of symbiosis.

COMPETENCY 018   **UNDERSTAND POPULATION DYNAMICS AND SPECIES DIVERSITY**

Skill 18.1   **Identifying factors that affect the growth rate and size of a population (e.g., carrying capacity, birthrate, migration)**

A **population** is a group of individuals of one species that live in the same general area. Many factors affect population size and growth rate. Population size can depend on the total amount of life a habitat can support. This is the **carrying capacity** of the environment. Once the habitat runs out of food, water, shelter, or space, the carrying capacity decreases, and then stabilizes.

FACTORS THAT AFFECT POPULATION GROWTH

Competition is when two or more species in a community use the same resources to live. Competition is usually detrimental to both populations. Competition is often difficult to find in nature, because competition between two populations is not continuous. Either the weaker population will cease to exist, or one population will evolve to utilize other available resources.

Limiting factors can affect population growth. As a population increases, competition for resources is more intense, and the growth rate declines. This is a **density-dependent** growth factor. The carrying capacity of an environment can be determined by the density-dependent factor. **Density-independent factors** affect individuals, regardless of population size. The weather and climate are good examples of density-independent factors. Temperatures that are too hot or cold can kill many individuals from a population that has not reached its carrying capacity.

MODELS OF POPULATION GROWTH

A zero population growth rate occurs when the birth and death rates in a population are equal. Exponential growth occurs when there is an abundance of resources and the growth rate is at its maximum, which is called the intrinsic rate of increase. This relationship can be graphically represented in a growth curve. An exponentially growing population begins with little change and then rapidly increases, as seen in the J-curve below.

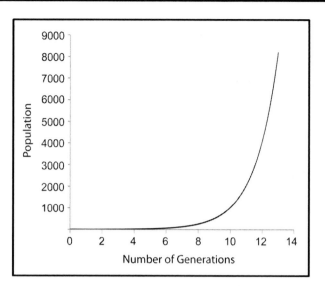

Logistic population growth incorporates the environment's carrying capacity into the growth rate. As a population reaches the carrying capacity, the growth rate begins to slow down and level off, as depicted in the S-curve below.

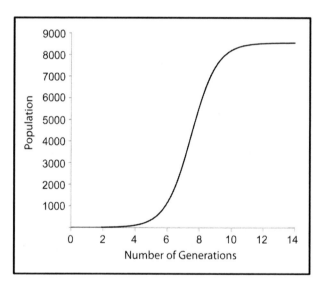

Many populations follow this model of population growth. Humans, however, are an exponentially growing population. Eventually, the carrying capacity of the Earth will be reached, and the growth rate will level off.

Skill 18.2   Applying knowledge of population dynamics and inter- and intraspecific relationships to explain or predict changes in population sizes of organisms for given changes in an ecosystem

Population dynamics are complex and most studies rely on mathematical modeling to estimate future trends based on known data points, with an emphasis on developing a model that matches historic population levels. In the simplistic models commonly used, such as the logistic population growth rate described in Skill 18.1, some factor or factors are used to impose an ultimate limit upon the population size. In stable populations, population size increase is only possible if this limit, or carrying capacity, is increased. Models can also take into account various biotic and abiotic factors that influence the population density, and these factors can be varied within the model.

Skill 18.3   Demonstrating knowledge of biotic and abiotic factors that influence the diversity of species in an ecosystem and of processes that lead to changes in species composition and diversity over time (e.g., succession)

The diversity of species in a particular ecosystem often depends upon the length of time that the ecosystem has been extant and stable. In classical theory, a new ecosystem arises from widespread disturbance, leaving an "open field" scenario where successive waves of species mixes exploit the ecosystem. For example, primary or pioneer species enjoy early successes, but later are displaced by secondary species. In this process, a climax community is eventually established, which is a species mix that is stable within the ecosystem and that is not displaced by other species mixes. This presupposes that the ecosystem does not vary over long periods of time. Other types of diversity cycle with seasons or other environmental factors.

FACTORS THAT INFLUENCE DIVERSITY OF SPECIES

Succession is an orderly process of replacing a community that has been damaged or has ceased to exist. Primary succession occurs where life never existed before; for example, in a flooded area or on a new volcanic island. Secondary succession takes place in communities that were once flourishing but were disturbed, but not totally stripped, by some cause, either manmade or natural. A climax community is a community that is established and flourishing.

Abiotic and Biotic Factors

Abiotic and biotic factors play a role in succession. **Biotic factors** are living things in an ecosystem (e.g., plants, animals, bacteria, and fungi). **Abiotic factors** are non-living aspects of an ecosystem (e.g., soil quality, rainfall, and temperature).

Abiotic factors affect succession by impacting which species can colonize an area. Certain species will or will not survive depending on the weather, climate, or soil makeup. Biotic factors, such as inhibition of one species due to another, may also be present. This is often due to some form of competition between the species.

SPECIES DIVERSITY AND RICHNESS

Species diversity is simply a count of the number of different species in a given area. A species is a group of plants or animals that are similar, and able to breed and produce viable offspring.

Biologists are unsure of how many different species live on the earth. Estimates range from 2 to 100 million. So far, only 2.1 million species have been classified. Most of these species live in the middle latitudes. Most of the species that remain unclassified are invertebrates. This group includes insects, spiders, worms, and crustaceans. It is difficult to classify invertebrates, because of their small size and the inaccessibility of the habitats in which they live. Another habitat that is relatively inaccessible is the tropical rain forest. It is estimated that this single biome may contain 50 - 90% of the Earth's biodiversity.

Many species have become extinct over the course of geological history. Driving factors for extinction include extreme fluctuations in the environment and increased competition from superior species. Because of the industrial revolution, a large number of biologically classified species have become extinct. The continued extinction of species caused by human activities is one of the greatest environmental problems we currently face.

Species diversity is one of the three categories of biodiversity. The other two are genetic diversity (the total number of genetic characteristics expressed and recessed in all of the individuals that comprise a particular species) and ecosystem diversity (the variation of habitats, community types, and non-living chemical and physical components in a given area).

Species richness is an important component of an ecosystem's biodiversity. Species richness is measurable in practice and has been found to be a good substitute for other measures of biodiversity that are difficult to measure.

A few facts about species richness:

1. Species richness is a measure of biodiversity.
2.
3. Species richness increases from high latitudes to low latitudes.
4. Maximal species richness occurs between 20 - 30° N latitude, which includes the tropics region.
5. Larger areas contain more species, because there are more opportunities for species to live there.
6. Generally, the relationship between species richness and a species being endemic to a specific area are positively correlated. However, there are some islands in which there is a high degree of endemism, but a low level of species richness.

Skill 18.4   Analyzing differences in population size and species diversity between various habitats, ecosystems, or biomes

An **ecosystem** is the collection of all components and processes that define a portion of the biosphere. Ecosystems include both biotic (living) and abiotic (non-living) components. While individual organisms in an ecosystem affect other members of the ecosystem, ecosystems themselves are also interrelated. Because the boundaries of ecosystems are not fixed, organisms and other ecosystem components can move freely between ecosystems. For example, the waste products from a terrestrial ecosystem may enter an aquatic ecosystem, changing its environmental characteristics. In addition, any ecosystem process that alters the global environment affects all the other ecosystems.

A **habitat** is the specific climactic and geographic region within an ecosystem exploited by a specific population. A **biome** is an abstract type of ecosystem, and the two terms often are used interchangeably. Similar ecosystems often have similar species diversity, though the particular species may vary. Two similar habitats should be able to support member of the same species. As with ecosystems, any process that alters a habitat or biome potentially affects population density and species diversity. This is one reason that habitat destruction poses such a serious threat to global species diversity.

COMPETENCY 019   UNDERSTAND THE CYCLING OF MATTER AND THE
                  FLOW OF ENERGY

Skill 19.1   Demonstrating knowledge of the cycling of a given substance (e.g.,
              carbon, nitrogen, phosphorus) through the living and nonliving
              components of the biosphere

Biogeochemical cycles are nutrient cycles that involve both biotic and abiotic factors.

TYPES OF BIOGEOCHEMICAL CYCLES

Water Cycle

Two percent of all the available water on Earth is fixed and unavailable in ice or the
bodies of organisms. Available water includes surface water (e.g., lakes, oceans, and
rivers) and ground water (e.g., aquifers and wells). Ninety six percent (96%) of all
available water is ground water. The water cycle is driven by solar energy. Water is
recycled through the processes of evaporation and precipitation. The water present now
is the water that has been here since Earth's atmosphere formed.

Carbon Cycle

Ten percent (10%) of all available carbon in the air (in the form of carbon dioxide gas) is
fixed by photosynthesis. Plants fix carbon in the form of glucose. Animals eat the plants
to obtain carbon. When animals release carbon dioxide through respiration, the plants
again have a source of carbon for further fixation.

Nitrogen Cycle

Eighty percent (80%) of the atmosphere is in the form of nitrogen gas. Nitrogen must be
fixed and taken out of its gaseous form to be incorporated into an organism. Only a few
genera of bacteria have the correct enzymes to break the triple bond between nitrogen
atoms in a process called nitrogen fixation. These bacteria live within the roots of
legumes (e.g., peas, beans, and alfalfa) and add nitrogen to the soil so it can be
absorbed by the plant. Nitrogen is necessary to make amino acids and the nitrogenous
bases of DNA.

Phosphorus Cycle

Phosphorus exists as a mineral and is not found in the atmosphere. A mutualistic
symbioses between fungi (Myco) and plant roots (rhiza) called mycorrhizae fixes
insoluble phosphates into useable phosphorus. Urine and decayed matter return
phosphorus to the earth, where it can be fixed in plants. Phosphorus is required for the
manufacture of ATP and DNA.

Skill 19.2   Analyzing the flow of energy both within a living system and between the system and the biosphere

Trophic levels are based on the feeding relationships that determine energy flow and chemical cycling. Autotrophs are the primary producers of the ecosystem. **Producers** consist primarily of plants. **Primary consumers** are the next trophic level. The primary consumers are the herbivores that eat plants or algae. **Secondary consumers** are the carnivores that eat the primary consumers. **Tertiary consumers** eat the secondary consumers. These trophic levels may go higher, depending on the ecosystem. **Decomposers** are consumers that feed on animal waste and dead organisms. This pathway of food transfer is depicted by a food chain.

Most food chains are more elaborate, becoming food webs. Energy is lost as the trophic levels progress from producer to tertiary consumer. The amount of energy that is transferred between trophic levels is called ecological efficiency. This energy flow is visually represented in a **pyramid of productivity**.

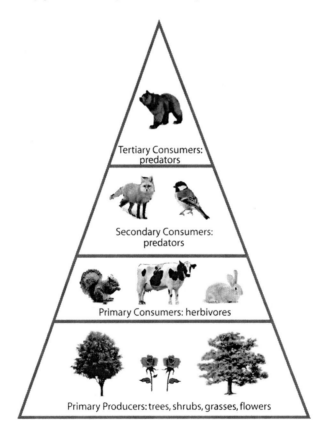

A **biomass pyramid** represents the total dry weight of organisms in each trophic level. A **pyramid of numbers** is a representation of the population size of each trophic level. The producers, being the most populous, are on the bottom of this pyramid, and the tertiary consumers, which are the least populous, are on the top.

Skill 19.3   Identifying the roles of various organisms (e.g., producers, decomposers) in the cycling of nutrients and flow of energy

Within a given system, chemical nutrients are repetitively cycled and energy flows through a network of organisms. Trophic levels are based on the feeding relationships that determine energy flow and chemical nutrient cycling. Autotrophs are the primary producers of the ecosystem, converting abiotic energy, such as sunlight, into chemical energy. **Producers** consist primarily of plants. **Primary consumers** are the next trophic level. The primary consumers are the herbivores that eat plants or algae. **Secondary consumers** are the carnivores that eat the primary consumers. **Tertiary consumers** eat the secondary consumers. **Decomposers** are consumers that feed on animal waste and dead organisms. This pathway of chemical nutrient and energy transfer is typically depicted by a food chain.

Decomposers recycle the carbon accumulated in durable organic material that does not immediately proceed to the carbon cycle. Ammonification is the decomposition of organic nitrogen back into ammonia. This process of the nitrogen cycle is carried out by aerobic and anaerobic bacterial and fungal decomposers. Decomposers add phosphorous back to the soil by decomposing the excretion of animals.

COMPETENCY 020   UNDERSTAND THE BEHAVIOR OF ORGANISMS

Skill 20.1   **Demonstrating knowledge of behaviors by which organisms respond to environmental changes or interact with organisms of their own and other species**

Most animals exhibit a fairly codified routine of behavior that does not vary widely among members of the species. Of course, some animals, particularly vertebrates, have complex behavioral repertoires. For this reason, most comprehensive studies of behavior focus on simpler organisms such as insects. Behaviors ultimately provide a boost to an organism's fitness and should be understood within that context. The study of animal behavior is called **ethology**. Ethological studies typically focus on four aspects of behavior—function, causation, development, and evolutionary history.

Skill 20.2   **Explaining or predicting the behavioral responses of an animal to a given set of interactions or environmental changes**

Animal behavior can be analyzed with an emphasis on proximate or ultimate causes. Proximate causes might be something like "the animal is cold and so seeks shelter," whereas ultimate causes will deal with an increase in fitness with relation to natural selection. Environmental changes or organism interactions will generally elicit a variety of responses that are suitable to the organism's capability and ecological niche. Studies of behavior often seek to codify a range of possible behaviors for a given organism or species and then establish predictive matrices based on given stimuli. Through these studies, fairly accurate predictions of behavior are possible.

Skill 20.3   **Analyzing behavioral responses of a given organism in terms of natural selection**

All studies of organism behavior should consider fitness costs and benefits of behavior as the ultimate cause of behaviors. For example, an organism does not hibernate because it is "sleepy," but rather because there is a fitness benefit to hibernation. Natural selection is the ultimate driver of all behavior—behaviors that increase fitness will become more common, while behaviors that decrease fitness will become less common. This does not mean that the study of proximate causes of behavior is not valuable.

Skill 20.4   **Demonstrating knowledge of methods for observing, measuring, and describing the physical behavior of animals**

Animal behavior is responsible for courtship leading to mating, communication between species, territoriality, aggression between animals, and dominance within a group. Animal communication is any behavior by one animal that affects the behavior of another animal. Animals use body language, sound, and smell to communicate.

Perhaps the most common type of animal communication is the presentation or movement of distinctive body parts. Many species of animals reveal or conceal body parts to communicate with potential mates, predators, and prey. In addition, many species of animals communicate with sound. Examples of vocal communication include the mating "songs" of birds and frogs and the warning cries of monkeys. Finally, many animals release scented chemicals to communicate with other animals. Pheromones are one class of scented chemicals that are important in reproduction and mating. Another class of distinctive odors, secreted from specialized glands, function to alert animals to the presence of others.

Innate behaviors are inborn or instinctual. An environmental stimulus, such as the length of day or temperature, results in an innate behavior. Hibernation among some animals is an innate behavior. **Learned behavior** is behavior that has been modified due to past experience.

Sample Test

Directions: Select the best answer in each group.

LIFE SCIENCE RESEARCH AND APPLICATIONS

1. Identify the control in the following experiment: A student grew four plants under the following conditions and measured photosynthetic rate by measuring mass. He grew two plants in 50% light and two plants in 100% light.
(Average) (Skill 1.1)

   A. Plants grown with no added nutrients

   B. Plants grown in the dark

   C. Plants grown in 100% light

   D. Plants grown in 50% light

2. In a data set, the value that occurs with the greatest frequency is referred to as the:
(Average) (Skill 1.2)

   A. Mean

   B. Median

   C. Mode

   D. Range

3. Three plants were grown and the following data recorded. Determine the mean growth.
(Easy) (Skill 1.2)

   Plant 1:   10 cm
   Plant 2:   20 cm
   Plant 3:   15 cm

   A. 5 cm

   B. 45 cm

   C. 12 cm

   D. 15 cm

4. In which of the following situations would a linear extrapolation of data be appropriate?
(Rigorous) (Skill 1.2)

   A. Computing the death rate of an emerging disease

   B. Computing the number of plant species in a forest over time

   C. Computing the rate of diffusion with a constant gradient

   D. Computing a population at equilibrium

5. **Paper chromatography is most often associated with the separation of:**
    (Average) (Skill 1.4)

    A. Nutritional elements

    B. DNA

    C. Proteins

    D. Plant pigments

6. **Which of the following is *not* usually found on the MSDS for a laboratory chemical?**
    (Rigorous) (Skill 1.5)

    A. Melting Point

    B. Toxicity

    C. Storage Instructions

    D. Cost

7. **Which item should always be used when using chemicals with noxious vapors?**
    (Easy) (Skill 1.5)

    A. Eye protection

    B. Face shield

    C. Fume hood

    D. Lab apron

8. **Which of the following limit the development of technological design ideas and solutions?**
    (Average) (Skill 1.6)

    I.   Monetary cost
    II.   Time
    III. Laws of nature
    IV.   Governmental regulation

    A. I and II

    B. I, II, and IV

    C. II and III

    D. I, II, and III

9. **Which of the following is the *least* ethical choice for a school laboratory activity?**
    (Rigorous) (Skill 1.6)

    A. Dissection of a donated cadaver

    B. Dissection of a preserved fetal pig

    C. Measuring the skeletal remains of birds

    D. Pithing a frog to watch the circulatory system

10. The three main concerns in nonrenewable resource management are conservation, environmental mitigation, and: *(Rigorous) (Skill 1.6)*

   A. Preservation

   B. Extraction

   C. Allocation

   D. Sustainability

11. The concept that the rate of a given process is controlled by the most scarce factor in the process is known as: *(Average) (Skill 3.1)*

   A. The Rate of Origination

   B. The Law of the Minimum

   C. The Law of Limitation

   D. The Law of Conservation

MOLECULAR AND CELLULAR LIFE PROCESSES

12. The shape of a cell depends on its: *(Average) (Skill 4.1)*

   A. Function

   B. Structure

   C. Age

   D. Size

13. Which type of cell would contain the most mitochondria? *(Average) (Skill 4.1)*

   A. Muscle cell

   B. Nerve cell

   C. Epithelial cell

   D. Blood cell

14. Which of the follow is *not* true of both chloroplasts and mitochondria? *(Easy) (Skill 4.1)*

   A. The inner membrane is the primary site for their activity.

   B. They convert energy from one form to another.

   C. They use an electron transport chain.

   D. They are important parts of the carbon cycle.

15. Which part of the cell is responsible for lipid synthesis? *(Rigorous) (Skill 4.1)*

   A. Golgi apparatus

   B. Rough endoplasmic reticulum

   C. Smooth endoplasmic reticulum

   D. Lysosome

16. **According to the fluid-mosaic model of the cell membrane, membranes are composed of:**
(Rigorous) (Skill 4.1)

    A.   A phospholipid bilayer with proteins embedded in the layers

    B.   One layer of phospholipids with cholesterol embedded in the layer

    C.   Two layers of protein with lipids embedded in the layers

    D.   DNA and fluid proteins

17. **A type of molecule *not* found in the membrane of an animal cell is:**
(Rigorous) (Skill 4.1)

    A.   Phospholipid

    B.   Protein

    C.   Cellulose

    D.   Cholesterol

18. **Which of the following is *not* considered evidence of the Endosymbiotic Theory?**
(Rigorous) (Skill 4.1)

    A.   The presence of genetic material in mitochondria and plastids

    B.   The presence of ribosomes within mitochondria and plastids

    C.   The presence of a double-layered membrane in mitochondria and plastids

    D.   The ability of mitochondria and plastids to reproduce

19. **The International System of Units (SI) measurement for temperature is on the _____ scale.**
(Rigorous) (Skill 4.2)

    A.   Celsius

    B.   Farenheit

    C.   Kelvin

    D.   Rankine

20. **If the niches of two species overlap, what usually results?**
(Easy) (Skill 5.1)

    A.   A symbiotic relationship

    B.   Cooperation

    C.   Competition

    D.   A new species

21. **Primary succession occurs after:**
(Average) (Skill 5.1)

A. Nutrient enrichment

B. A forest fire

C. Exposure of a bare rock after the water table permanently recedes

D. A housing development is built

22. **A clownfish is protected by the sea anemone's tentacles. In turn, the anemone receives uneaten food from the clownfish. This is an example of:**
(Easy) (Skill 5.1)

A. Mutualism

B. Parasitism

C. Commensalism

D. Competition

23. **Which of the following are reasons to maintain biological diversity?**
(Rigorous) (Skill 5.1)

I. Consumer product development
II. Stability of the environment
III. Habitability of our planet
IV. Cultural diversity

A. I and III

B. II and III

C. I, II, and III

D. I, II, III, and IV

24. **Which of the following is *not* an abiotic factor?**
(Easy) (Skill 5.1)

A. Temperature

B. Rainfall

C. Soil quality

D. Bacteria

25. **The loss of an electron is _____ and the gain of an electron is _____.**
(Rigorous) (Skill 5.4)

A. oxidation, reduction

B. reduction, oxidation

C. glycolysis, photosynthesis

D. photosynthesis, glycolysis

26. **During the Krebs cycle, 8 carrier molecules are formed. What are they?**
(Rigorous) (Skill 5.4)

   A.   3 NADH, 3 FADH, 2 ATP

   B.   6 NADH and 2 ATP

   C.   4 $FADH_2$ and 4 ATP

   D.   6 NADH and 2 $FADH_2$

27. **The product of anaerobic respiration in animals is:**
(Average) (Skill 5.4)

   A.   Carbon dioxide

   B.   Lactic acid

   C.   Pyruvate

   D.   Ethyl alcohol

28. **What is necessary for diffusion to occur?**
(Average) (Skill 6.1)

   A.   Carrier proteins

   B.   Energy

   C.   A concentration gradient

   D.   A membrane

29. **ATP is known to bind to phosphofructokinase-1 (an enzyme involved in glycolysis). This results in a change in the shape of the enzyme that causes the rate of ATP production to fall. Which answer best describes this phenomenon?**
(Rigorous) (Skill 6.4)

   A.   Binding of a coenzyme

   B.   An allosteric change in the enzyme

   C.   Competitive inhibition

   D.   Uncompetitive inhibition

MOLECULAR REPRODUCTION AND HEREDITY

30. **Identify this stage of mitosis.**
(Average) (Skill 7.1)

   A.   Anaphase

   B.   Metaphase

   C.   Telophase

   D.   Prophase

31. **Which statement regarding mitosis is correct?**
(Easy) (Skill 7.1)

    A.   Diploid cells produce haploid cells for sexual reproduction.

    B.   Sperm and egg cells are produced.

    C.   Diploid cells produce diploid cells for growth and repair.

    D.   It allows for greater genetic diversity.

32. **This stage of mitosis includes cytokinesis, or division of the cytoplasm and its organelles.**
(Average) (Skill 7.1)

    A.   Anaphase

    B.   Interphase

    C.   Prophase

    D.   Telophase

33. **Replication of chromosomes occurs during which phase of the cell cycle?**
(Average) (Skill 7.1)

    A.   Prophase

    B.   Interphase

    C.   Metaphase

    D.   Anaphase

34. **Which process(es) result(s) in a haploid chromosome number?**
(Easy) (Skill 7.4)

    A.   Both meiosis and mitosis

    B.   Mitosis

    C.   Meiosis

    D.   Replication and division

35. **Crossing over, which increases genetic diversity, occurs during which stage(s)?**
(Rigorous) (Skill 7.4)

    A.   Telophase II in meiosis

    B.   Metaphase in mitosis

    C.   Interphase in both mitosis and meiosis

    D.   Prophase I in meiosis

36. **The Law of Segregation defined by Mendel states that:**
    (Average) (Skill 8.1)

    A. When sex cells form, the two alleles that determine a trait will end up on different gametes

    B. Only one of two alleles is expressed in a heterozygous organism

    C. The allele expressed is the dominant allele

    D. Alleles of one trait do not affect the inheritance of alleles on another chromosome

37. **A child with type O blood has a father with type A blood and a mother with type B blood. The genotypes of the parents, respectively, would be which of the following?**
    (Average) (Skill 8.1)

    A. AA and BO

    B. AO and BO

    C. AA and BB

    D. AO and OO

38. **A woman has Pearson Syndrome, a disease caused by a mutation in mitochondrial DNA. In which of the following individuals would you expect to see the disease?**
    (Rigorous) (Skill 8.1)

    I   Her Daughter
    II Her Son
    III Her Daughter's son
    IV Her Son's daughter

    A. I, III

    B. I, II, III

    C. II, IV

    D. I, II, III, IV

39. **Which is not a possible effect of polyploidy?**
    (Rigorous) (Skill 8.1)

    A. More robust members of an animal species

    B. The creation of cross-species offspring

    C. The creation of a new species

    D. Cells that produce higher levels of desired proteins

40. Based on the pedigree chart below, what term best describes the nature of the trait being mapped?
(Rigorous) (Skill 8.1)

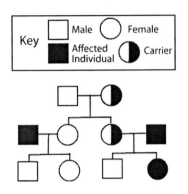

A.   Autosomal recessive

B.   Sex-linked

C.   Incomplete dominance

D.   Co-dominance

41. Segments of DNA can be transferred from one organism to another through the use of which of the following?
(Average) (Skill 9.1)

A.   Bacterial plasmids

B.   Viruses

C.   Chromosomes from frogs

D.   Plant DNA

42. Which of the following is *not* a form of posttranscriptional processing?
(Rigorous) (Skill 9.1)

A.   5' capping

B.   Intron splicing

C.   Polypeptide splicing

D.   3' polyadenylation

43. Which of the following carries amino acids to the ribosome in protein synthesis?
(Average) (Skill 9.1)

A.   Messenger RNA

B.   Ribosomal RNA

C.   Transfer RNA

D.   DNA

44. A DNA molecule has the sequence ACTATG. What is the anticodon of this molecule?
(Rigorous) (Skill 9.1)

A.   UGAUAC

B.   ACUAUG

C.   TGATAC

D.   ACTATG

45. **Viruses are made of:**
    (Easy) (Skill 9.2)

    A.   A protein coat surrounding
          nucleic acid

    B.   DNA, RNA, and a cell wall

    C.   Nucleic acid surrounding a
          protein coat

    D.   Protein surrounded by DNA

46. **Which of the following is not a
    useful application of genetic
    engineering?**
    (Rigorous) (Skill 10.1)

    A.   The creation of safer viral
          vaccines

    B.   The creation of bacteria
          that produce hormones for
          medical use

    C.   The creation of bacteria to
          break down toxic waste

    D.   The creation of organisms
          that are successfully being
          used as sources for
          alternative fuels

47. **Which of the following is a way
    that cDNA cloning has not been
    used?**
    (Rigorous) (Skill 10.2)

    A.   To provide evidence for
          taxonomic organization

    B.   To study the mutations that
          lead to diseases such as
          hemophilia

    C.   To determine the structure
          of a protein

    D.   To understand methods of
          gene regulation

48. **A genetic engineering
    advancement in the medical
    field is:**
    (Easy) (Skill 10.2)

    A.   Gene therapy

    B.   Pesticides

    C.   Degradation of harmful
          chemicals

    D.   Antibiotics

49. **Genetic engineering is beneficial to agriculture in many ways. Which of the following is *not* an advantage of genetic engineering in the field of agriculture?**
(Average) (Skill 10.3)

    A.   Use of bovine growth hormone to increase milk production

    B.   Development of crops resistant to herbicides

    C.   Development of microorganisms to break down toxic substances into harmless compounds

    D.   Genetic vaccination of plants against viral attack

50. **The demand for genetically enhanced crops has increased in recent years. Which of the following is *not* a reason for this increased demand?**
(Easy) (Skill 10.3)

    A.   Fuel sources

    B.   Increased growth

    C.   Insect resistance

    D.   Better-looking produce

51. **Stewardship is the responsible management of resources. We must regulate our actions to do which of the following about environmental degradation?**
(Average) (Skill 10.3)

    A.   Prevent it

    B.   Reduce it

    C.   Mitigate it

    D.   All of the above

STRUCTURAL AND FUNCTIONAL RELATIONSHIPS

52. **The scientific name Canis familiaris refers to the animal's:**
(Easy) (Skill 11.2)

    A.   Kingdom and phylum names

    B.   Genus and species names

    C.   Class and species names

    D.   Order and family names

53. **Thermoacidophiles are:**
(Average) (Skill 11.2)

    A.   Prokaryotes

    B.   Eukaryotes

    C.   Protists

    D.   Archaea

54. **Protists are classified into major groups according to:**
(Average) (Skill 11.2)

A. Their method of obtaining nutrition

B. Reproduction

C. Metabolism

D. Their form and function

55. **All of the following are examples of a member of Kingdom Fungi except:**
(Easy) (Skill 11.2)

A. Mold

B. Algae

C. Mildew

D. Mushrooms

56. **Which kingdom is comprised of organisms made of one cell with no nuclear membrane?**
(Easy) (Skill 11.2)

A. Monera

B. Protista

C. Fungi

D. Algae

57. **Within the Phylum Mollusca there are examples of both open and closed circulatory systems. Which of the following is a feature that is *not* common to both the open and closed cirulatory systems of molluscs?**
(Rigorous) (Skill 11.2)

A. Hemocoel

B. Plasma

C. Vessels

D. Heart

58. **Which of the following systems considers Archea (or Archeabacteria) as the most inclusive level of the taxonomic system?**
(Rigorous) (Skill 11.2)

I   Three domain system
II   Five kingdom system
III Six kingdom system
IV   Eight kingdom system

A. II, III

B. I, IV

C. I, III, IV

D. I, II, III, IV

59. **Laboratory researchers distinguish fungi from plants and classify them differently because the cell walls of fungi contain:**
(Rigorous) (Skill 11.2)

A. Chitin

B. Lignin

C. Lipopolysaccharides

D. Cellulose

60. **Which phylum accounts for 85% of all animal species?**
(Easy) (Skill 11.2)

A. Nematoda

B. Chordata

C. Arthropoda

D. Cnidaria

61. **Fats are broken down by which substance?**
(Average) (Skill 11.2)

A. Bile produced in the gall bladder

B. Lipase produced in the gall bladder

C. Glucagons produced in the liver

D. Bile produced in the liver

62. **Identify the correct characteristics of the plant pictured below.**
(Rigorous) (Skill 12.1)

A. Seeded, non-vascular

B. Non-seeded, vascular

C. Non-seeded, non-vascular

D. Seeded, vascular

63. **Which of the following is a characteristic of a monocot?**
(Rigorous) (Skill 12.1)

A. Parallel veins in leaves

B. Flower petals occurring in multiples of four or five

C. Two seed leaves

D. Vascular tissue absent from the stem

64. **Spores are the reproductive mode for which of the following group of plants?**
(Average) (Skill 12.1)

A.   Algae

B.   Flowering plants

C.   Conifers

D.   Ferns

65. **Using the following taxonomic key, identify the tree from which the branch below came.**
(Rigorous) (Skill 12.1)

1 - Are the leaves PALMATELY COMPOUND (BLADES arranged like fingers on a hand)? – go to question 2
1 - Are the leaves PINNATELY COMPOUND (BLADES arranged like the vanes of a feather)? – go to question 3

2 - Are there usually 7 BLADES - Aesculus hippocastanum
2 - Are there usually 5 BLADES - Aesculus glabra

3 - Are there mostly 3-5 BLADES that are LOBED or coarsely toothed? - Acer negundo
3 - Are there mostly 5-13 BLADES with smooth or toothed edges? - Fraxinus Americana

A.   Aesculus hippocastanum

B.   Aesculus glabra

C.   Acer negundo

D.   Fraxinus Americana

66. **Which of the following is *not* a factor that affects the rate of both photosynthesis and respiration in plants?**
(Average) (Skill 12.1)

A. The concentration of NADP and FAD

B. The temperature

C. The structure of the plant's leaves

D. The availability of different substrates

67. **Oxygen is given off in the:**
(Easy) (Skill 12.1)

A. Light reaction of photosynthesis

B. Dark reaction of photosynthesis

C. Krebs cycle

D. Reduction of NAD^+ to NADH

68. **The most ATP is generated through:**
(Rigorous) (Skill 12.1)

A. Fermentation

B. Glycolysis

C. Chemiosmosis

D. The Krebs cycle

69. **Which of the following is *not* employed by a young cactus to survive in an arid environment?**
(Rigorous) (Skill 12.1)

A. Stem as the principle site of photosynthesis

B. A deep root system to reach additional sources of groundwater

C. CAM cycle photosynthesis

D. Spherical growth form

70. **Oxygen created in photosynthesis comes from the breakdown of:**
(Average) (Skill 12.1)

A. Carbon dioxide

B. Water

C. Glucose

D. Carbon monoxide

71. **A plant cell is placed in salt water. The resulting movement of water out of the cell is called:**
(Average) (Skill 12.1)

A. Facilitated diffusion

B. Diffusion

C. Transpiration

D. Osmosis

72. **Movement is possible by the action of muscles pulling on:**
    (Average) (Skill 12.2)

    A.   Skin

    B.   Bones

    C.   Joints

    D.   Ligaments

73. **Hormones are essential for the regulation of reproduction. What organ is responsible for the release of hormones for sexual maturity?**
    (Average) (Skill 12.2)

    A.   Pituitary gland

    B.   Hypothalamus

    C.   Pancreas

    D.   Thyroid gland

74. **Which of the following compounds is *not* needed for skeletal muscle contraction to occur?**
    (Rigorous) (Skill 12.2)

    A.   Glucose

    B.   Sodium

    C.   Acetylcholine

    D.   Adenosine 5'-triphosphate

75. **Which of the following hormones is most involved in the process of osmoregulation?**
    (Rigorous) (Skill 12.2)

    A.   Antidiuretic Hormone

    B.   Melatonin

    C.   Calcitonin

    D.   Gulcagon

76. **Capillaries come into contact with a large surface of both the kidneys and the lungs, especially in relation to the volume of these organs. Which of the following is *not* true of both organs and their contact with capillaries?**
    (Rigorous) (Skill 12.2)

    A.   Small specialized sections of each organ contact capillaries

    B.   A large branching system of tubes within the organ

    C.   A large source of blood that is quickly divided into capillaries

    D.   A sack that contains a capillary network

77. **Which of the following substances in unlikely to cause negative consequences if over-ingested?**
(Rigorous) (Skill 12.2)

   A.   Essential fatty acids

   B.   Essential minerals

   C.   Essential water-insoluble vitamins

   D.   Essential water-soluble vitamins

78. **If someone were experiencing unexplained changes in body temperature, hunger level, and circadian rythyms, which of the following structures would most likely be the cause of these problems?**
(Rigorous) (Skill 12.2)

   A.   Hypothalamus

   B.   Central nervous system

   C.   Pineal gland

   D.   Basal ganglia

79. **A boy had the chicken pox as a baby. He will most likely not get this disease again because of:**
(Average) (Skill 13.1)

   A.   Passive immunity

   B.   Vaccination

   C.   Antibiotics

   D.   Active immunity

80. **Cancer cells divide extensively and invade other tissues. This continuous cell division is due to:**
(Rigorous) (Skill 13.3)

   A.   Density-dependent inhibition

   B.   Density-independent inhibition

   C.   Chromosome replication

   D.   Growth factors

DIVERSITY AND BIOLOGICAL EVOLUTION

81. **Man's scientific name is Homo sapiens. Choose the proper classification, beginning with kingdom and ending with order.**
(Average) (Skill 14.1)

   A.   Animalia, Vertebrata, Mammalia, Primate, Hominidae

   B.   Animalia, Vertebrata, Chordata, Homo sapiens

   C.   Animalia, Chordata, Vertebrata, Mammalia, Primate

   D.   Chordata, Vertebrata, Primate, Homo sapiens

82. **The two major ways to determine taxonomic classification are:**
(Average) (Skill 14.1)

    A.   Evolution and phylogeny

    B.   Reproductive success and evolution

    C.   Phylogeny and morphology

    D.   Size and color

83. **Which of the following best exemplifies the Theory of Inheritance of Acquired Traits?**
(Average) (Skill 15.1)

    A.   Giraffes need to reach higher for leaves to eat, so their necks stretch. The giraffe babies are then born with longer necks. Eventually, there are more long-necked giraffes in the population.

    B.   Giraffes with longer necks are able to reach more leaves, so they eat more and have more babies than the other giraffes. Eventually, there are more long-necked giraffes in the population.

    C.   Giraffes want to reach higher for leaves to eat, so they release enzymes into their bloodstream, which in turn cause fetal development of longer-necked giraffes. Eventually, there are more long-necked giraffes in the population.

    D.   Giraffes with long necks are more attractive to other giraffes, so they get the best mating partners and produce more babies. Eventually, there are more long-necked giraffes in the population.

84. **Evolution occurs in:**
(Easy) (Skill 15.2)

   A.   Individuals

   B.   Populations

   C.   Organ systems

   D.   Cells

85. **Which of the following factors will affect the Hardy-Weinberg law of equilibrium, leading to evolutionary change?**
(Average) (Skill 15.2)

   A.   No mutations

   B.   Non-random mating

   C.   No immigration or emigration

   D.   Large population

86. **If a population is in Hardy-Weinberg equilibrium and the frequency of the recessive allele is 0.3, what percentage of the population would be expected to be heterozygous?**
(Rigorous) (Skill 15.2)

   A.   9%

   B.   49%

   C.   42%

   D.   21%

87. **An animal choosing its mate because of attractive plumage or a strong mating call is an example of:**
(Average) (Skill 15.2)

   A.   Sexual selection

   B.   Natural selection

   C.   Mechanical isolation

   D.   Linkage

88. **Which of the following is an example of a phenotype that gives the organism an advantage in its home environment?**
(Rigorous) (Skill 15.2)

   A.   The color of Pepper Moths in England

   B.   Thornless roses in a nature perserve

   C.   Albinism in naked mole rats

   D.   The large thorax of a Mediterranean fruit fly

89. **Members of the same species:**
(Easy) (Skill 15.2)

   A.   Look identical

   B.   Never change

   C.   Reproduce successfully within their group

   D.   Live in the same geographic location

90. **Reproductive isolation results in:**
(Average) (Skill 15.2)

    A. Extinction

    B. Migration

    C. Follilization

    D. Speciation

91. **The biological species concept applies to:**
(Average) (Skill 15.2)

    A. Asexual organisms

    B. Extinct organisms

    C. Sexual organisms

    D. Fossil organisms

92. **Which aspect of science does not support evolution?**
(Average) (Skill 16.1)

    A. Comparative anatomy

    B. Organic chemistry

    C. Comparison of DNA among organisms

    D. Analogous structures

93. **Any change that affects the sequence of nucleotides in a gene is called a:**
(Easy) (Skill 16.2)

    A. Deletion

    B. Polyploid

    C. Mutation

    D. Duplication

94. The fossil record is often cited as providing evidence for the theory of punctuated equilibrium. Which of the following examples can only be explained by punctuated equilibrium and not gradualism?
(Rigorous) (Skill 16.2)

    I   Coelacanth fish (once thought extinct) have remained relatively unchanged for millions of years.

    II   The sudden apearance of a large number of different soft-bodied animals around 530 million years ago

    III   10-million-year-old fossils and modern ginko plants are nearly identical.

    IV   Fossils of Red Deer from the Island of Jersey show a six-fold decrease in body weight over the last 6,000 years.

A. I, III

B. II, IV

C. I, II, III, IV

D. None of the above

95. What is convergent evolution?
(Average) (Skill 16.3)

A. The development of closely related species

B. The development of unrelated species that do not share similar biological structures

C. The development of similar biological structures in similar species

D. The development of similar biological structures in unrelated (or distantly related) species

INTERDEPENDENCE AND BEHAVIOR OF ORGANISMS

96. What is commensalism?
(Easy) (Skill 17.2)

A. One predator eating another species as its prey

B. One species benefiting from the another without causing any harm to the other species

C. Competition for resources such as habitat, food, and mates

D. One predator species living on or in another species causing detrimental effects to the host

97. The first cells that evolved on earth were probably of which type?
(Average) (Skill 18.1)

    A.   Autotrophs

    B.   Eukaryotes

    C.   Heterotrophs

    D.   Prokaryotes

98. All of the following are density-dependent factors that affect a population except:
(Rigorous) (Skill 18.1)

    A.   Disease

    B.   Drought

    C.   Predation

    D.   Migration

99. Which of the following is *not* an example of dynamic equilibrium?
(Rigorous) (Skill 18.1)

    A.   A stable population

    B.   A symbiotic pair of organisms

    C.   Osmoregulation

    D.   Maintaining head position while walking

100. All of the following are density-independent factors that affect a population except:
(Average) (Skill 18.1)

    A.   Temperature

    B.   Rainfall

    C.   Predation

    D.   Soil nutrients

Answer Key

1. C	35. D	69. B
2. C	36. A	70. B
3. D	37. B	71. B
4. C	38. B	72. B
5. D	39. A	73. B
6. D	40. B	74. A
7. C	41. A	75. A
8. D	42. C	76. D
9. D	43. C	77. D
10. C	44. B	78. A
11. B	45. A	79. D
12. A	46. D	80. B
13. A	47. C	81. C
14. A	48. A	82. C
15. C	49. C	83. A
16. A	50. D	84. B
17. C	51. D	85. B
18. C	52. B	86. C
19. C	53. D	87. A
20. C	54. D	88. A
21. C	55. B	89. C
22. A	56. A	90. D
23. D	57. A	91. C
24. D	58. C	92. B
25. A	59. A	93. C
26. D	60. C	94. D
27. B	61. D	95. D
28. C	62. B	96. B
29. B	63. A	97. D
30. B	64. D	98. B
31. C	65. C	99. D
32. D	66. C	100. C
33. B	67. A	
34. C	68. C	

Rigor Table

	Easy 20%	Average Rigor 40%	Rigorous 40%
Question	3, 7, 14, 20, 22, 24, 31, 34, 45, 48, 50, 52, 55, 56, 60, 67, 84, 89, 93, 96	1, 2, 5, 8, 11, 12, 13, 21, 27, 28, 30, 32, 33, 36, 37, 41, 43, 49, 51, 53, 54, 61, 64, 66, 70, 71, 72, 73, 79, 81, 82, 83, 85, 87, 90, 91, 92, 95, 97, 100	4, 6, 9, 10, 15, 16, 17, 18, 19, 23, 25, 26, 29, 35, 38, 39, 40, 42, 44, 46, 47, 57, 58, 59, 62, 63, 65, 68, 69, 74, 75, 76, 77, 78, 80, 86, 88, 94, 98, 99

Rationales with Sample Questions

Directions: Select the best answer in each group.

LIFE SCIENCE RESEARCH AND APPLICATIONS

1.   Identify the control in the following experiment: A student grew four plants under the following conditions and measured photosynthetic rate by measuring mass. He grew two plants in 50% light and two plants in 100% light.
(Average) (Skill 1.1)

   A.   Plants grown with no added nutrients

   B.   Plants grown in the dark

   C.   Plants grown in 100% light

   D.   Plants grown in 50% light

Answer: C. Plants grown in 100% light.
The plants grown in 100% light are the control with which the student will compare the growth of the plants 50% light.

2.   In a data set, the value that occurs with the greatest frequency is referred to as the:
(Average) (Skill 1.2)

   A.   Mean

   B.   Median

   C.   Mode

   D.   Range

Answer: C. Mode
The mode is the value that occurs the most often in a set of data. A data set is bimodal if there are two values that occur with equal frequency.

3. **Three plants were grown and the following data recorded. Determine the mean growth.**
(Easy) (Skill 1.2)

Plant 1:   **10 cm**
Plant 2:   **20 cm**
Plant 3:   **15 cm**

A.   5 cm

B.   45 cm

C.   12 cm

D.   15 cm

Answer: D. 15 cm
The mean growth is the average of the three growth heights.

$$\frac{10 + 20 + 15}{3} = 15 \text{ cm average height}$$

4. **In which of the following situations would a linear extrapolation of data be appropriate?**
(Rigorous) (Skill 1.2)

A.   Computing the death rate of an emerging disease

B.   Computing the number of plant species in a forest over time

C.   Computing the rate of diffusion with a constant gradient

D.   Computing a population at equilibrium

Answer: C: Computing the rate of diffusion with a constant gradient
The individual data points on a linear graph cluster around a line of best fit. In other words, a relationship is linear if we can sketch a straight line that roughly fits the data points. Extrapolation is the process of estimating data points outside a known set of data points. When extrapolating data of a linear relationship, we extend the line of best fit beyond the known values. The extension of the line represents the estimated data points. Extrapolating data is only appropriate if we are relatively certain that the relationship is indeed linear.

5. **Paper chromatography is most often associated with the separation of:**
    (Average) (Skill 1.4)

    A. Nutritional elements

    B. DNA

    C. Proteins

    D. Plant pigments

Answer: D. Plant pigments
Paper chromatography uses the principles of capillarity to separate substances such as plant pigments. Molecules of a larger size will move more slowly up the paper, whereas smaller molecules will move more quickly, producing lines of pigment.

6. **Which of the following is *not* usually found on the MSDS for a laboratory chemical?**
    (Rigorous) (Skill 1.5)

    A. Melting Point

    B. Toxicity

    C. Storage Instructions

    D. Cost

Answer: D. Cost
MSDSs, or Material Safety Data Sheets, are used to make sure that anyone can easily obtain information about a chemical, especially in the event of a spill or accident. This information typically includes physical data, toxicity, health effects, first aid, reactivity, storage, disposal, protective measures, and spill/leak procedures. Cost is not generally included on MSDSs. Costs are generated by the distributor, and seperate suppliers can have different costs.

7. **Which item should always be used when using chemicals with noxious vapors?**
    (Easy) (Skill 1.5)

    A.   Eye protection

    B.   Face shield

    C.   Fume hood

    D.   Lab apron

Answer: C. Fume hood
Fume hoods are designed to protect the experimenter from chemical fumes. The three other choices do not prevent chemical fumes from entering the respiratory system.

8. **Which of the following limit the development of technological design ideas and solutions?**
    (Average) (Skill 1.6)

    V.   **Monetary cost**
    VI.   **Time**
    VII.   **Laws of nature**
    VIII. **Governmental regulation**

    A.   I and II

    B.   I, II, and IV

    C.   II and III

    D.   I, II, and III

Answer: D. I, II, and III
Technology cannot work against the laws of nature. Technological design solutions must work within the framework of the natural world. Monetary cost and time constraints also limit the development of new technologies. Governmental regulation, while present in many scientific fields, cannot regulate the formation of new ideas or design solutions.

9. **Which of the following is the *least* ethical choice for a school laboratory activity?**
   (Rigorous) (Skill 1.6)

   A.   Dissection of a donated cadaver

   B.   Dissection of a preserved fetal pig

   C.   Measuring the skeletal remains of birds

   D.   Pithing a frog to watch the circulatory system

Answer: D. Pithing a frog to watch the circulatory system
Scientific and societal ethics make choosing experiments in today's science classroom difficult. It is possible to ethically perform choices (A), (B), or (C), if due care is taken. (Note that students will need significant assistance and maturity to perform these experiments, and that due care also means attending to all legal paperwork that might be necessary.) However, modern practice precludes pithing animals (causing partial brain death while allowing some systems to function) as inhumane.

10. **The three main concerns in nonrenewable resource management are conservation, environmental mitigation, and:**
    (Rigorous) (Skill 1.6)

    A.   Preservation

    B.   Extraction

    C.   Allocation

    D.   Sustainability

Answer: C. Allocation
The main concerns in nonrenewable resource management are conservation, allocation, and environmental mitigation. Policymakers, corporations, and governments must determine how to use and distribute scarce resources. Decision makers balance the immediate demand for resources with the need for resources in the future. This determination is often a cause of conflict and disagreement. Finally, scientists attempt to minimize and mitigate the environmental damage caused by resource extraction.

11.   **The concept that the rate of a given process is controlled by the most scarce factor in the process is known as:**
       (Average) (Skill 3.1)

      A.   The Rate of Origination

      B.   The Law of the Minimum

      C.   The Law of Limitation

      D.   The Law of Conservation

Answer: B. The Law of the Minimum
A limiting factor is the component of a biological process that determines how quickly or slowly the process proceeds. Photosynthesis is the main biological process determining the rate of ecosystem productivity, or the rate at which an ecosystem creates biomass. Thus, in evaluating the productivity of an ecosystem, potential limiting factors are light intensity, gas concentrations, and mineral availability. The Law of the Minimum states that the required factor that is most scarce in a given process controls the rate of the process.

MOLECULAR AND CELLULAR LIFE PROCESSES

12.   **The shape of a cell depends on its:**
       (Average) (Skill 4.1)

      A.   Function

      B.   Structure

      C.   Age

      D.   Size

Answer: A. Function
In most living organisms, cellular structure is based on function.

13. **Which type of cell would contain the most mitochondria?**
   (Average) (Skill 4.1)

   A. Muscle cell

   B. Nerve cell

   C. Epithelial cell

   D. Blood cell

Answer: A. Muscle cell
Mitochondria are the site of cellular respiration, where ATP is produced. Muscle cells have the most mitochondria because they use a great deal of energy.

14. **Which of the follow is *not* true of both chloroplasts and mitochondria?**
   (Easy) (Skill 4.1)

   A. The inner membrane is the primary site for their activity.

   B. They convert energy from one form to another.

   C. They use an electron transport chain.

   D. They are important parts of the carbon cycle.

Answer: A. The inner membrane is the primary site for their activity.
In mitochondria the electron transport chain is present in the inner membrane; however, in chloroplasts it is present in the thylakoid membranes.

15. **Which part of the cell is responsible for lipid synthesis?**
   (Rigorous) (Skill 4.1)

   A. Golgi apparatus

   B. Rough endoplasmic reticulum

   C. Smooth endoplasmic reticulum

   D. Lysosome

Answer: C. Smooth endoplasmic reticulum
The rough endoplasmic reticulum and the golgi apparatus are both involved in the production of proteins (synthesis and packaging, respectively). Lysosomes contain digestive enzymes. Only the smooth endoplasmic reticulum is directly responsible for lipid production.

16. **According to the fluid-mosaic model of the cell membrane, membranes are composed of:**
    (Rigorous) (Skill 4.1)

    A.   A phospholipid bilayer with proteins embedded in the layers

    B.   One layer of phospholipids with cholesterol embedded in the layer

    C.   Two layers of protein with lipids embedded in the layers

    D.   DNA and fluid proteins

Answer: A. Phospholipid bilayers with proteins embedded in the layers
Cell membranes are composed of a phospholipid bilayer in which hydrophilic heads face outward and hydrophobic tails are sandwiched between the hydrophilic layers. The membrane contains proteins embedded in the layer (integral proteins) and proteins on the surface (peripheral proteins).

17. **A type of molecule *not* found in the membrane of an animal cell is:**
    (Rigorous) (Skill 4.1)

    A.   Phospholipid

    B.   Protein

    C.   Cellulose

    D.   Cholesterol

Answer: C. Cellulose
Phospholipids, protein, and cholesterol are all found in animal cells. Cellulose, however, is only found in plant cells.

18. Which of the following is *not* considered evidence of the Endosymbiotic Theory?
(Rigorous) (Skill 4.1)

  A. The presence of genetic material in mitochondria and plastids

  B. The presence of ribosomes within mitochondria and plastids

  C. The presence of a double-layered membrane in mitochondria and plastids

  D. The ability of mitochondria and plastids to reproduce

Answer: C. The presence of a double-layered membrane in mitochondria and plastids.
A double-layered membrane is not unique to mitochondria and plastids; the nucleus is also double-layered. All three other characteristics are not present in any other organelle, and are evidence that mitochondria and plastids may once have been separate organisms.

19. The International System of Units (SI) measurement for temperature is on the _____ scale.
(Rigorous) (Skill 4.2)

  A. Celsius

  B. Farenheit

  C. Kelvin

  D. Rankine

Answer: C. Kelvin
Science uses the SI system because of its worldwide acceptance and ease of comparison. The SI scale for measuring temperature is the Kelvin Scale. Science, however, uses the Celsius scale for its ease of use.

20. **If the niches of two species overlap, what usually results?**
(Easy) (Skill 5.1)

    A.   A symbiotic relationship

    B.   Cooperation

    C.   Competition

    D.   A new species

Answer: C. Competition
Two species that occupy the same habitat or eat the same food are said to be in competition with one another.

21. **Primary succession occurs after:**
(Average) (Skill 5.1)

    A.   Nutrient enrichment

    B.   A forest fire

    C.   Exposure of a bare rock after the water table permanently recedes

    D.   A housing development is built

Answer: C. Exposure of a bare rock after the water table permanently recedes
Primary succession occurs where life never existed before, such as flooded areas or a new volcanic island. It is only after the water recedes that the rock is able to support new life.

22. **A clownfish is protected by the sea anemone's tentacles. In turn, the anemone receives uneaten food from the clownfish. This is an example of:** *(Easy) (Skill 5.1)*

    A. Mutualism

    B. Parasitism

    C. Commensalism

    D. Competition

Answer: A. Mutualism

Neither the clownfish nor the anemone harms the other; they both benefit from their relationship. Mutualism is when two species that occupy a similar space both benefit from their relationship.

23. **Which of the following are reasons to maintain biological diversity?** *(Rigorous) (Skill 5.1)*

    V. **Consumer product development**
    VI. **Stability of the environment**
    VII. **Habitability of our planet**
    VIII. **Cultural diversity**

    A. I and III

    B. II and III

    C. I, II, and III

    D. I, II, III, and IV

Answer: D. I, II, III, and IV

Biological diversity refers to the extraordinary variety of living things and ecological communities on Earth. Maintaining biological diversity is important for many reasons. First, we derive many consumer products from living organisms in nature. Second, the stability and habitability of the environment depends on the varied contributions of many different organisms. Finally, the cultural traditions of human populations depend on the diversity of the natural world.

24. **Which of the following is *not* an abiotic factor?**
    (Easy) (Skill 5.1)

    A.   Temperature

    B.   Rainfall

    C.   Soil quality

    D.   Bacteria

Answer: D. Bacteria
Abiotic factors are the non-living aspects of an ecosystem. Bacteria is an example of a biotic factor, a living thing.

25. **The loss of an electron is _____ and the gain of an electron is _____.**
    (Rigorous) (Skill 5.4)

    A.   oxidation, reduction

    B.   reduction, oxidation

    C.   glycolysis, photosynthesis

    D.   photosynthesis, glycolysis

Answer: A. oxidation, reduction
Oxidation-reduction reactions are also known as redox reactions. In respiration, energy is released by the transfer of electrons in redox reactions. The oxidation phase of this reaction involves the loss of an electron, and the reduction phase involves the gain of an electron.

26. **During the Krebs cycle, 8 carrier molecules are formed. What are they? (Rigorous) (Skill 5.4)**

    A.   3 NADH, 3 FADH, 2 ATP

    B.   6 NADH and 2 ATP

    C.   4 $FADH_2$ and 4 ATP

    D.   6 NADH and 2 $FADH_2$

Answer: D. 6 NADH and 2 $FADH_2$
For each molecule of CoA that enters the Kreb's cycle, you get 3 NADH and 1 $FADH_2$. There are 2 molecules of CoA, so the total yield is 6 NADH and 2 $FADH_2$ during the Krebs cycle.

27. **The product of anaerobic respiration in animals is: (Average) (Skill 5.4)**

    A.   Carbon dioxide

    B.   Lactic acid

    C.   Pyruvate

    D.   Ethyl alcohol

Answer: B. Lactic acid
In anaerobic lactic acid fermentation, pyruvate is reduced by NADH to form lactic acid. This is the anaerobic process in animals. Alcoholic fermentation is an anaerobic process in yeast and some bacteria, which yields ethyl alcohol. Carbon dioxide and pyruvate are products of aerobic respiration.

28. **What is necessary for diffusion to occur?**
    (Average) (Skill 6.1)

    A.   Carrier proteins

    B.   Energy

    C.   A concentration gradient

    D.   A membrane

Answer: C. A concentration gradient
Diffusion is the ability of molecules to move from areas of high concentration to areas of low concentration (a concentration gradient).

29. **ATP is known to bind to phosphofructokinase-1 (an enzyme involved in glycolysis). This results in a change in the shape of the enzyme that causes the rate of ATP production to fall. Which answer best describes this phenomenon?**
    (Rigorous) (Skill 6.4)

    A.   Binding of a coenzyme

    B.   An allosteric change in the enzyme

    C.   Competitive inhibition

    D.   Uncompetitive inhibition

Answer: B. An allosteric change in the enzyme
The binding of ATP to phosphofructokinase-1 causes an allosteric change (a change in shape) of the enzyme. The binding of ATP can be considered non-competitive inhibition.

MOLECULAR REPRODUCTION AND HEREDITY

30. **Identify this stage of mitosis.**
    (Average) (Skill 7.1)

    A.   Anaphase

    B.   Metaphase

    C.   Telophase

    D.   Prophase

Answer: B. Metaphase
During metaphase, the centromeres are at opposite ends of the cell. During this phase, the chromosomes are aligned with one another in the middle of the cell.

31. **Which statement regarding mitosis is correct?**
    (Easy) (Skill 7.1)

    A.   Diploid cells produce haploid cells for sexual reproduction.

    B.   Sperm and egg cells are produced.

    C.   Diploid cells produce diploid cells for growth and repair.

    D.   It allows for greater genetic diversity.

Answer: C. Diploid cells produce diploid cells for growth and repair.
The purpose of mitotic cell division is to provide growth and repair in body (somatic) cells. The cells begin as diploid and produce diploid cells.

32. **This stage of mitosis includes cytokinesis, or division of the cytoplasm and its organelles.**
    (Average) (Skill 7.1)

    A.   Anaphase

    B.   Interphase

    C.   Prophase

    D.   Telophase

Answer: D. Telophase
The last stage of the mitosis is telophase. Here, the two nuclei form with a full set of DNA each. The cell is pinched in half into two cells, and cytokinesis, or the division of the cytoplasm and organelles, occurs.

33. **Replication of chromosomes occurs during which phase of the cell cycle?**
    (Average) (Skill 7.1)

    A.   Prophase

    B.   Interphase

    C.   Metaphase

    D.   Anaphase

Answer: B. Interphase
Interphase is the stage where the cell grows and copies the chromosomes in preparation for the mitotic phase.

34. **Which process(es) result(s) in a haploid chromosome number?**
    (Easy) (Skill 7.4)

    A.   Both meiosis and mitosis

    B.   Mitosis

    C.   Meiosis

    D.   Replication and division

Answer: C. Meiosis
In meiosis, there are two consecutive cell divisions, resulting in the reduction of chromosome number by half (diploid to haploid).

35. **Crossing over, which increases genetic diversity, occurs during which stage(s)?**
(Rigorous) (Skill 7.4)

    A.   Telophase II in meiosis

    B.   Metaphase in mitosis

    C.   Interphase in both mitosis and meiosis

    D.   Prophase I in meiosis

Answer: D. Prophase I in meiosis
During prophase I of meiosis, the replicated chromosomes condense and pair with their homologues in a process called synapsis. Crossing over, the exchange of genetic material between homologues, occurs during prophase I.

36. **The Law of Segregation defined by Mendel states that:**
(Average) (Skill 8.1)

    A.   When sex cells form, the two alleles that determine a trait will end up on different gametes

    B.   Only one of two alleles is expressed in a heterozygous organism

    C.   The allele expressed is the dominant allele

    D.   Alleles of one trait do not affect the inheritance of alleles on another chromosome

Answer: A. When sex cells form, the two alleles that determine a trait will end up on different gametes
The law of segregation states that the two alleles of each trait segregate to different gametes.

37. **A child with type O blood has a father with type A blood and a mother with type B blood. The genotypes of the parents, respectively, would be which of the following?**
(Average) (Skill 8.1)

   A. AA and BO

   B. AO and BO

   C. AA and BB

   D. AO and OO

Answer: B. AO and BO
Type O blood has 2 recessive O genes. A child receives one allele from each parent; therefore, each parent in this example must have an O allele. The father has type A blood with a genotype of AO, and the mother has type B blood with a genotype of BO.

38. **A woman has Pearson Syndrome, a disease caused by a mutation in mitochondrial DNA. In which of the following individuals would you expect to see the disease?**
(Rigorous) (Skill 8.1)

   I   Her Daughter
   II   Her Son
   III   Her Daughter's son
   IV   Her Son's daughter

   A. I, III

   B. I, II, III

   C. II, IV

   D. I, II, III, IV

Answer: B. I, II, III
Because mitochondrial DNA is passed through the maternal line, both of her children would be affected, and the trait would continue to pass from her daughter to all of the daughter's children. Her son's children would recieve their mitochondrial DNA from their mother.

39.   **Which is not a possible effect of polyploidy?**
       (Rigorous) (Skill 8.1)

       A.   More robust members of an animal species

       B.   The creation of cross-species offspring

       C.   The creation of a new species

       D.   Cells that produce higher levels of desired proteins

Answer: A. More robust members of an animal species
While polyploidy often creates new plant species, thereby yeilding more robust crops, it is likely to create nonviable animal offspring.

40.   **Based on the pedigree chart below, what term best describes the nature of the trait being mapped?**
       (Rigorous) (Skill 8.1)

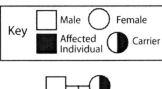

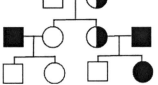

       A.   Autosomal recessive

       B.   Sex-linked

       C.   Incomplete dominance

       D.   Co-dominance

Answer: B. Sex-linked
This chart would be a good example of color blindness, a sex-linked trait. If the trait had been autosomal recessive, the last generation would all be carriers, with the exception of the affected individual. In the case of traits that are incompletely dominant or co-dominant the tree would require additional notation.

41. **Segments of DNA can be transferred from one organism to another through the use of which of the following?**
(Average) (Skill 9.1)

A. Bacterial plasmids

B. Viruses

C. Chromosomes from frogs

D. Plant DNA

Answer: A. Bacterial plasmids
Plasmids can transfer themselves (and therefore their genetic information) through a process called conjugation. This requires cell-to-cell contact.

42. **Which of the following is *not* a form of posttranscriptional processing?**
(Rigorous) (Skill 9.1)

A. 5' capping

B. Intron splicing

C. Polypeptide splicing

D. 3' polyadenylation

Answer: C. Polypeptide splicing
The removal of segments of polypeptides is a posttranslational process. The other three answer choices are methods of posttranscriptional processing.

43. **Which of the following carries amino acids to the ribosome in protein synthesis?**
(Average) (Skill 9.1)

    A.   Messenger RNA

    B.   Ribosomal RNA

    C.   Transfer RNA

    D.   DNA

Answer: C. Transfer RNA
The tRNA molecule is specific for a particular amino acid. The tRNA has an anticodon sequence that is complementary to the codon. This specifies where the tRNA places the amino acid in protein synthesis.

44. **A DNA molecule has the sequence ACTATG. What is the anticodon of this molecule?**
(Rigorous) (Skill 9.1)

    A.   UGAUAC

    B.   ACUAUG

    C.   TGATAC

    D.   ACTATG

Answer: B. ACUAUG
The DNA is first transcribed into mRNA. Here, the DNA has the sequence ACTATG; therefore, the complementary mRNA sequence is UGAUAC (remember, in RNA, T is U). This mRNA sequence is the codon. The anticodon is the complement to the codon. The anticodon sequence will be ACUAUG (remember, the anticodon is tRNA, so U is present instead of T).

45.   **Viruses are made of:**
       (Easy) (Skill 9.2)

       A.   A protein coat surrounding nucleic acid

       B.   DNA, RNA, and a cell wall

       C.   Nucleic acid surrounding a protein coat

       D.   Protein surrounded by DNA

Answer: A. A protein coat surrounding nucleic acid
Viruses are composed of a protein coat and nucleic acid; either RNA or DNA.

46.   **Which of the following is not a useful application of genetic engineering?**
       (Rigorous) (Skill 10.1)

       A.   The creation of safer viral vaccines

       B.   The creation of bacteria that produce hormones for medical use

       C.   The creation of bacteria to break down toxic waste

       D.   The creation of organisms that are successfully being used as sources for
             alternative fuels

Answer: D. The creation of organisms that are successfully being used as a source alternative fuels
Although there is a push to genetically engineer organisms that will either create alternative fuels or be used as an alternative fuel source, this field is in its infancy. There are multiple successful examples for each of the other posssible answers.

47. **Which of the following is a way that cDNA cloning has not been used?** *(Rigorous) (Skill 10.2)*

    A.   To provide evidence for taxonomic organization

    B.   To study the mutations that lead to diseases such as hemophilia

    C.   To determine the structure of a protein

    D.   To understand methods of gene regulation

Answer: C. To determine the structure of a protein
Although cDNA cloning can be used to determine the amino acid sequence of a protein, many other steps determine the final protein structure, for example, the folding of the protein, addition of other protein subunits, and/or modification by other proteins.

48. **A genetic engineering advancement in the medical field is:** *(Easy) (Skill 10.2)*

    A.   Gene therapy

    B.   Pesticides

    C.   Degradation of harmful chemicals

    D.   Antibiotics

Answer: A. Gene therapy
Gene therapy is the introduction of a normal allele into somatic cells in order to replace a defective gene. The medical field has had success in treating patients with a single-enzyme deficiency disease. Gene therapy has allowed doctors and scientists to introduce a normal allele that provides the missing enzyme.

49. Genetic engineering is beneficial to agriculture in many ways. Which of the following is *not* an advantage of genetic engineering in the field of agriculture?
(Average) (Skill 10.3)

    A. Use of bovine growth hormone to increase milk production

    B. Development of crops resistant to herbicides

    C. Development of microorganisms to break down toxic substances into harmless compounds

    D. Genetic vaccination of plants against viral attack

Answer: C. Development of microorganisms to break down toxic substances into harmless compounds
All of the answers are actual results of genetic engineering; however, only answer (C) has not been used for agricultural purposes. These microorganisms have, however, been used at toxic waste sites and oil spills.

50. The demand for genetically enhanced crops has increased in recent years. Which of the following is *not* a reason for this increased demand?
(Easy) (Skill 10.3)

    A. Fuel sources

    B. Increased growth

    C. Insect resistance

    D. Better-looking produce

Answer: D. Better-looking produce
Genetically enhanced crops are being developed for utilization as fuel sources, as well as for an increased production yield. Insect resistance eliminates the need for pesticides. While there may be some farmers crossing crops to make prettier watermelons, this is not a primary reason for the increased demand.

51.   **Stewardship is the responsible management of resources. We must regulate our actions to do which of the following about environmental degradation?**
       (Average) (Skill 10.3)

       A.   Prevent it

       B.   Reduce it

       C.   Mitigate it

       D.   All of the above

Answer: D. All of the above
Stewardship requires the regulation of human activity to prevent, reduce, and mitigate environmental degradation. An important aspect of stewardship is the preservation of resources and ecosystems for future human generations.

STRUCTURAL AND FUNCTIONAL RELATIONSHIPS

52.   **The scientific name Canis familiaris refers to the animal's:**
       (Easy) (Skill 11.2)

       A.   Kingdom and phylum names

       B.   Genus and species names

       C.   Class and species names

       D.   Order and family names

Answer: B. Genus and species names
Each species is scientifically known by a two-part name, a system called binomial nomenclature. The first word in the name is the genus and the second word is its specific epithet (species name).

53. **Thermoacidophiles are:**
    (Average) (Skill 11.2)

    A.   Prokaryotes

    B.   Eukaryotes

    C.   Protists

    D.   Archaea

Answer: D. Archaea
Thermoacidophiles, methanogens, and halobacteria are members of the archaea group. They are as different from prokaryotes as prokaryotes are from eukaryotes.

54. **Protists are classified into major groups according to:**
    (Average) (Skill 11.2)

    A.   Their method of obtaining nutrition

    B.   Reproduction

    C.   Metabolism

    D.   Their form and function

Answer: D. Their form and function
The extreme variation in protist classification reflects their diverse forms, functions, and lifestyles. The protists are often grouped as algae (plant-like), protozoa (animal-like), or fungus-like, based on the similarity of their characteristics.

55. **All of the following are examples of a member of Kingdom Fungi except:**
    (Easy) (Skill 11.2)

    A.   Mold

    B.   Algae

    C.   Mildew

    D.   Mushrooms

Answer: B. Algae
Mold, mildew, and mushrooms are all fungi. Brown and golden algae are members of the Kingdom Protista and green algae are members of the Plant Kingdom.

56. **Which kingdom is comprised of organisms made of one cell with no nuclear membrane?**
(Easy) (Skill 11.2)

    A.   Monera

    B.   Protista

    C.   Fungi

    D.   Algae

Answer: A. Monera
Monera is the only kingdom comprising unicellular organisms lacking a nucleus. Algae are classified as a protist. Algae may be uni- or multicellular and have a nucleus.

57. **Within the Phylum Mollusca there are examples of both open and closed circulatory systems. Which of the following is a feature that is *not* common to both the open and closed cirulatory systems of molluscs?**
(Rigorous) (Skill 11.2)

    A.   Hemocoel

    B.   Plasma

    C.   Vessels

    D.   Heart

Answer: A. Hemocoel
Hemocoel is the blood-filled cavity that is present in animals with open circulatory systems. Unlike some other open circulatory systems, the molluscs have three blood vessels, two to bring blood from the lungs and one to push blood into the hemocoel.

58. **Which of the following systems considers Archea (or Archeabacteria) as the most inclusive level of the taxonomic system?**
    (Rigorous) (Skill 11.2)

I	Three domain system
II	Five kingdom system
III	Six kingdom system
IV	Eight kingdom system

    A.   II, III

    B.   I, IV

    C.   I, III, IV

    D.   I, II, III, IV

Answer: C. I, III, IV
In the five kingdom system, the subkingdom Archaebacteriobionta is under the kingdom Monera.

59. **Laboratory researchers distinguish fungi from plants and classify them differently because the cell walls of fungi contain:**
    (Rigorous) (Skill 11.2)

    A.   Chitin

    B.   Lignin

    C.   Lipopolysaccharides

    D.   Cellulose

Answer: A. Chitin
All of the possible answers are compounds found in cell walls. Cellulose is found in the cell wall of all plants, while lignin is found only in the cell wall of vascular plants. Lipopolysaccharides are found in the cell wall of gram-negative bacteria. Chitin is the only compound uniquely found in fungal cell walls.

60.   **Which phylum accounts for 85% of all animal species?**
      (Easy) (Skill 11.2)

      A.   Nematoda

      B.   Chordata

      C.   Arthropoda

      D.   Cnidaria

Answer: C. Arthropoda
The arthropoda phylum consists of insects, crustaceans, and spiders. They are the largest group in the animal kingdom.

61.   **Fats are broken down by which substance?**
      (Average) (Skill 11.2)

      A.   Bile produced in the gall bladder

      B.   Lipase produced in the gall bladder

      C.   Glucagons produced in the liver

      D.   Bile produced in the liver

Answer: D. Bile produced in the liver
The liver produces bile, which breaks down and emulsifies fatty acids.

62.   Identify the correct characteristics of the plant pictured below.
       (Rigorous) (Skill 12.1)

       A.   Seeded, non-vascular

       B.   Non-seeded, vascular

       C.   Non-seeded, non-vascular

       D.   Seeded, vascular

Answer: B. Non-seeded, vascular
The picture above is of a fern, Division Pterophyta, which is a spore-bearing vascular plant.

63.   Which of the following is a characteristic of a monocot?
       (Rigorous) (Skill 12.1)

       A.   Parallel veins in leaves

       B.   Flower petals occurring in multiples of four or five

       C.   Two seed leaves

       D.   Vascular tissue absent from the stem

Answer: A. Parallel veins in leaves
Monocots have one cotelydon, parallel veins in their leaves, and their flower petals are in multiples of threes. Dicots have flower petals in multiples of fours and fives.

64. **Spores are the reproductive mode for which of the following group of plants?**
    (Average) (Skill 12.1)

    A. Algae

    B. Flowering plants

    C. Conifers

    D. Ferns

Answer: D. Ferns
Ferns are non-seeded vascular plants. All plants in this group have spores and require water for reproduction. Algae, flowering plants, and conifers are not in this group of plants.

65. Using the following taxonomic key, identify the tree from which the branch below came.
(Rigorous) (Skill 12.1)

1 - Are the leaves PALMATELY COMPOUND (BLADES arranged like fingers on a hand)? – go to question 2
1 - Are the leaves PINNATELY COMPOUND (BLADES arranged like the vanes of a feather)? – go to question 3

2 - Are there usually 7 BLADES - Aesculus hippocastanum
2 - Are there usually 5 BLADES - Aesculus glabra

3 - Are there mostly 3-5 BLADES that are LOBED or coarsely toothed? - Acer negundo
3 - Are there mostly 5-13 BLADES with smooth or toothed edges? - Fraxinus Americana

A.   Aesculus hippocastanum

B.   Aesculus glabra

C.   Acer negundo

D.   Fraxinus Americana

Answer: C. Acer negundo
The leaves are pinnately compound, with 5 coarsly toothed leaves, leading to the answer: Acer negundo. The list below includes the scientific name and the common name for the all the plants listed above:
Aesculus hippocastanum (Horsechestnut)
Aesculus glabra (Ohio Buckeye)
Acer negundo (Boxelder, Ashleaf Maple)
Fraxinus Americana (White Ash)

66. **Which of the following is *not* a factor that affects the rate of both photosynthesis and respiration in plants?**
(Average) (Skill 12.1)

    A.   The concentration of NADP and FAD

    B.   The temperature

    C.   The structure of the plant's leaves

    D.   The availability of different substrates

Answer: C. The structure of plant's leaves
The structure of the plant's leaaves affects its ability to absorb light, which affects the rate of photosynthesis but not the rate of respiration.

67. **Oxygen is given off in the:**
(Easy) (Skill 12.1)

    A.   Light reaction of photosynthesis

    B.   Dark reaction of photosynthesis

    C.   Krebs cycle

    D.   Reduction of NAD^+ to NADH

Answer: A. Light reaction of photosynthesis
The conversion of solar energy to chemical energy occurs in light reactions. As chlorophyll absorbs light, electrons are transferred and cause water to split, releasing oxygen as a waste product.

68.   **The most ATP is generated through:**
      (Rigorous) (Skill 12.1)

      A.   Fermentation

      B.   Glycolysis

      C.   Chemiosmosis

      D.   The Krebs cycle

Answer: C. Chemiosmosis
The electron transport chain uses electrons to pump hydrogen ions across the mitochondrial membrane. This ion gradient is used to form ATP in a process called chemiosmosis. ATP is generated by the removal of hydrogen ions from NADH and $FADH_2$. This yields 34 ATP molecules.

69.   **Which of the following is *not* employed by a young cactus to survive in an arid environment?**
      (Rigorous) (Skill 12.1)

      A.   Stem as the principle site of photosynthesis

      B.   A deep root system to reach additional sources of groundwater

      C.   CAM cycle photosynthesis

      D.   Spherical growth form

Answer: B. A deep root system to reach additional sources of groundwater
A waxy sperical stem as the site of photosynthesis is an adaptation that limits water loss and allows for maximum water storage. CAM cycle photosynthesis allows the plant to open its stomata at night, thus limiting possible water loss due to evaporation. Some cacti will develop a taproot when it is necessary to stabilize the plant.

70. **Oxygen created in photosynthesis comes from the breakdown of:**
    (Average) (Skill 12.1)

    A. Carbon dioxide

    B. Water

    C. Glucose

    D. Carbon monoxide

Answer: B. Water
In photosynthesis, water is split; the hydrogen atoms are pulled to carbon dioxide, which is taken in by the plant and ultimately reduced to make glucose. The oxygen from water is given off as a waste product.

71. **A plant cell is placed in salt water. The resulting movement of water out of the cell is called:**
    (Average) (Skill 12.1)

    A. Facilitated diffusion

    B. Diffusion

    C. Transpiration

    D. Osmosis

Answer: B. Diffusion
Osmosis is simply the diffusion of water across a semi-permeable membrane. Water will diffuse out of the cell if less water is present on the outside than on the inside of the cell.

72. **Movement is possible by the action of muscles pulling on:**
    (Average) (Skill 12.2)

    A. Skin

    B. Bones

    C. Joints

    D. Ligaments

Answer: B. Bones
Skeletal muscles are attached to bones and are responsible for their movement.

73. **Hormones are essential for the regulation of reproduction. What organ is responsible for the release of hormones for sexual maturity?**
    (Average) (Skill 12.2)

    A.   Pituitary gland

    B.   Hypothalamus

    C.   Pancreas

    D.   Thyroid gland

Answer: B. Hypothalamus
The hypothalamus begins secreting hormones that help mature the reproductive system and stimulate development of secondary sex characteristics.

74. **Which of the following compounds is *not* needed for skeletal muscle contraction to occur?**
    (Rigorous) (Skill 12.2)

    A.   Glucose

    B.   Sodium

    C.   Acetylcholine

    D.   Adenosine 5'-triphosphate

Answer: A. Glucose
Although glucose is necessary to generate ATP (Adenosine 5'-triphosphate), it is not directly involved in muscular contractions. Acetylocholine is the neurotransmitter that intiates muscle contraction. Sodium plays an essential part in creating an action potential. Lastly, ATP provides the energy for contraction.

75. **Which of the following hormones is most involved in the process of osmoregulation?**
(Rigorous) (Skill 12.2)

    A.   Antidiuretic Hormone

    B.   Melatonin

    C.   Calcitonin

    D.   Gulcagon

Answer: A. Antidiuretic Hormone
The mechanism through which the body controls water concentration and various soluble materials is called osmoregulation. Antidiuretic Hormone (ADH) regulates the kidneys' reabsorption of water and directly affects the amount of water in the body. A failure to produce ADH can cause an individual to die from dehydration within a matter of hours. Calcitonin controls the removal of calcium from the blood. Glucagon, like insulin, controls the amount of glucose in the blood. Like ADH, melatonin plays a role in homeostasis by regulating body rhythms.

76. **Capillaries come into contact with a large surface of both the kidneys and the lungs, especially in relation to the volume of these organs. Which of the following is *not* true of both organs and their contact with capillaries? (Rigorous) (Skill 12.2)**

    A.   Small specialized sections of each organ contact capillaries

    B.   A large branching system of tubes within the organ

    C.   A large source of blood that is quickly divided into capillaries

    D.   A sack that contains a capillary network

Answer: D. A sack that contains a capillary network
The Bowmen's capsule of the kidneys can be described as a sack that contains a capillary network. The alveoli of the lungs are sacks, however, the capillaries are on the outside of the alveoli.

77. **Which of the following substances in unlikely to cause negative consequences if over-ingested?**
(Rigorous) (Skill 12.2)

    A.   Essential fatty acids

    B.   Essential minerals

    C.   Essential water-insoluble vitamins

    D.   Essential water-soluble vitamins

Answer: D. Essential water-soluble vitamins
Water-soluble vitamins are often removed in the filtration process by the kidneys and thus rarely build up to dangerous levels. Too many fatty acids can lead to obesity and other health problems. Excessive minerals can lead to a variety of different conditions, depending on the mineral ingested. Water-insoluble vitamins are usually stored in fatty tissues and thus are not flushed from the body. Therefore, water-insoluble vitamins can build up and reach dangerous levels.

78. **If someone were experiencing unexplained changes in body temperature, hunger level, and circadian rythyms, which of the following structures would most likely be the cause of these problems?**
(Rigorous) (Skill 12.2)

    A.   Hypothalamus

    B.   Central nervous system

    C.   Pineal gland

    D.   Basal ganglia

Answer: A. Hypothalamus
The pineal gland releases melatonin, which has been linked to sleep/wake patterns. The basal ganglia and central nervous system are structures regulating nerve impulses. Only the hypothalamus is responsible for regulating body temperature, hunger, and sleep/wake cycles.

79. **A boy had the chicken pox as a baby. He will most likely not get this disease again because of:**
(Average) (Skill 13.1)

      A.   Passive immunity

      B.   Vaccination

      C.   Antibiotics

      D.   Active immunity

Answer: D. Active immunity
Active immunity develops after recovery from an infectious disease, such as the chicken pox, or after vaccination. Passive immunity can be passed from one individual to another (from mother to nursing child).

80. **Cancer cells divide extensively and invade other tissues. This continuous cell division is due to:**
(Rigorous) (Skill 13.3)

      A.   Density-dependent inhibition

      B.   Density-independent inhibition

      C.   Chromosome replication

      D.   Growth factors

Answer: B. Density-independent inhibition
Density-dependent inhibition is when the cells crowd one another and consume all the nutrients, thereby halting cell division. Cancer cells, however, are density independent, meaning they can divide continuously as long as nutrients are present.

DIVERSITY AND BIOLOGICAL EVOLUTION

81.   **Man's scientific name is Homo sapiens. Choose the proper classification, beginning with kingdom and ending with order.**
        (Average) (Skill 14.1)

        A.   Animalia, Vertebrata, Mammalia, Primate, Hominidae

        B.   Animalia, Vertebrata, Chordata, Homo, sapiens

        C.   Animalia, Chordata, Vertebrata, Mammalia, Primate

        D.   Chordata, Vertebrata, Primate, Homo, sapiens

Answer: C. Animalia, Chordata, Vertebrata, Mammalia, Primate
The order of classification for humans is as follows: Kingdom, Animalia; Phylum, Chordata; Subphylum, Vertebrata; Class, Mammalia; Order, Primate; Family, Hominadae; Genus, Homo; Species, sapiens.

82.   **The two major ways to determine taxonomic classification are:**
        (Average) (Skill 14.1)

        A.   Evolution and phylogeny

        B.   Reproductive success and evolution

        C.   Phylogeny and morphology

        D.   Size and color

Answer: C. Phylogeny and morphology
Taxonomy is based on structure (morphology) and evolutionary relationships (phylogeny).

83. **Which of the following best exemplifies the Theory of Inheritance of Acquired Traits?**
(Average) (Skill 15.1)

A. Giraffes need to reach higher for leaves to eat, so their necks stretch. The giraffe babies are then born with longer necks. Eventually, there are more long-necked giraffes in the population.

B. Giraffes with longer necks are able to reach more leaves, so they eat more and have more babies than the other giraffes. Eventually, there are more long-necked giraffes in the population.

C. Giraffes want to reach higher for leaves to eat, so they release enzymes into their bloodstream, which in turn cause fetal development of longer-necked giraffes. Eventually, there are more long-necked giraffes in the population.

D. Giraffes with long necks are more attractive to other giraffes, so they get the best mating partners and produce more babies. Eventually, there are more long-necked giraffes in the population.

Answer: A. Giraffes need to reach higher for leaves to eat, so their necks stretch. The giraffe babies are then born with longer necks. Eventually, there are more long-necked giraffes in the population.
The theory of inheritance of acquired traits states that the offspring of an individual will benefit from the adaptations of the parent. The stretching of the neck thus leads to longer-necked offspring. Answer B best exemplifies the theory of natural selection, where an outside factor affects the chances of an individual to live and reproduce, and thus pass on its genetic material to the next generation. There is no evidence of desire creating genetic or developmental change in a fetus. Additionally there is no evidence that giraffes select mates based on neck length; however, if they did, this would be an example of sexual selection, an aspect of natural selection.

84. Evolution occurs in:
(Easy) (Skill 15.2)

    A.   Individuals

    B.   Populations

    C.   Organ systems

    D.   Cells

Answer: B. Populations.
Evolution is a change in genotype over time. Gene frequencies shift and change from generation to generation. Populations evolve, not individuals.

85. Which of the following factors will affect the Hardy-Weinberg law of equilibrium, leading to evolutionary change?
(Average) (Skill 15.2)

    A.   No mutations

    B.   Non-random mating

    C.   No immigration or emigration

    D.   Large population

Answer: B. Non-random mating
There are five requirements to maintain Hardy-Weinberg equilibrium: no mutation, no selection pressures, an isolated population, a large population, and random mating.

86. **If a population is in Hardy-Weinberg equilibrium and the frequency of the recessive allele is 0.3, what percentage of the population would be expected to be heterozygous?**
(Rigorous) (Skill 15.2)

    A.   9%

    B.   49%

    C.   42%

    D.   21%

Answer: C. 42%
0.3 is the value of q. Therefore, $q^2 = 0.09$. According to the Hardy-Weinberg equation, $1 = p + q$.

$1 = p + 0.3$.
$p = 0.7$
$p^2 = 0.49$

Next, plug q^2 and p^2 into the equation $1 = p^2 + 2pq + q^2$.

$1 = 0.49 + 2pq + 0.09$ (where $2pq$ is the number of heterozygotes)
$1 = 0.58 + 2pq$
$2pq = 0.42$

Multiply by 100 to get the percent of heterozygotes, 42%.

87. **An animal choosing its mate because of attractive plumage or a strong mating call is an example of:**
(Average) (Skill 15.2)

    A.   Sexual selection

    B.   Natural selection

    C.   Mechanical isolation

    D.   Linkage

Answer: A. Sexual selection
Sexual selection, the act of choosing a mate, allows animals to have some choice in the genetic makeup of their offspring.

88. **Which of the following is an example of a phenotype that gives the organism an advantage in its home environment?**
    (Rigorous) (Skill 15.2)

    A. The color of Pepper Moths in England

    B. Thornless roses in a nature perserve

    C. Albinism in naked mole rats

    D. The large thorax of a Mediterranean fruit fly

Answer: A. The color of Pepper Moths in England
Thornless roses are not naturally occuring and would not have an advantage against natural predators. Albinism is not any more common in naked mole rats than other species, and would not be advantageous in a subterrian environment. Thorax size in Mediterranean fruit flies has been linked to sexual selection; however, sexual selection is not an environmental pressure. The Pepper Moth of England is the most often-cited example of natural selection. A dramatic shift in color frequency occured during the industrial revolution. This color change occurred because moths camouflage on trees, and during the industrial revolution soot changed the color of trees.

89. **Members of the same species:**
    (Easy) (Skill 15.2)

    A. Look identical

    B. Never change

    C. Reproduce successfully within their group

    D. Live in the same geographic location

Answer: C. Reproduce successfully within their group
Species are defined by the ability to successfully reproduce with members of their own kind.

90.   **Reproductive isolation results in:**
        (Average) (Skill 15.2)

   A.   Extinction

   B.   Migration

   C.   Follilization

   D.   Speciation

Answer: D. Speciation
Reproductive isolation is caused by any factor that impedes two species from producing viable, fertile hybrids. Reproductive isolation of populations is the primary criterion for recognition of species status.

91.   **The biological species concept applies to:**
        (Average) (Skill 15.2)

   A.   Asexual organisms

   B.   Extinct organisms

   C.   Sexual organisms

   D.   Fossil organisms

Answer: C. Sexual organisms
The biological species concept states that a species is a reproductive community of populations that occupy a specific niche in nature. It focuses on reproductive isolation of populations as the primary criterion for recognition of species status. The biological species concept does not apply to organisms that are completely asexual in their reproduction, fossil organisms, or distinctive populations that hybridize.

92. **Which aspect of science does not support evolution?**
(Average) (Skill 16.1)

    A.   Comparative anatomy

    B.   Organic chemistry

    C.   Comparison of DNA among organisms

    D.   Analogous structures

Answer: B. Organic chemistry
Comparative anatomy is the comparison of anatomical characteristics among different species. This includes the study of homologous and analogous structures. The comparison of DNA between species is the best way to establish evolutionary relationships. The study of organic chemistry does not aid in the study of evolution.

93. **Any change that affects the sequence of nucleotides in a gene is called a:**
(Easy) (Skill 16.2)

    A.   Deletion

    B.   Polyploid

    C.   Mutation

    D.   Duplication

Answer: C. Mutation
A mutation is an inheritable change in DNA. It can be an error in replication or a spontaneous rearrangement of one ore more segments of DNA. Deletion and duplication are types of mutations. Polyploidy is when an organism has more than two complete sets of chromosomes.

94. The fossil record is often cited as providing evidence for the theory of punctuated equilibrium. Which of the following examples can only be explained by punctuated equilibrium and not gradualism?
(Rigorous) (Skill 16.2)

I   Coelacanth fish (once thought extinct) have remained relatively unchanged for millions of years.

II   The sudden apearance of a large number of different soft-bodied animals around 530 million years ago

III 10-million-year-old fossils and modern ginko plants are nearly identical.

IV   Fossils of Red Deer from the Island of Jersey show a six-fold decrease in body weight over the last 6,000 years.

A. I, III

B. II, IV

C. I, II, III, IV

D. None of the above

Answer: D. None of the above

Gradualism and punctuated equilibrium are not mutually exclusive. Because we are talking in terms of geological time, a rapid change can be thought to occur over a period of 1,000 years to 100,000 years or more. Items I and III appear to demonstrate a state of stasis; however, it is possible that some changes cannot be observed in the fossil record. Items II and IV appear to show a period of sudden change. In the case of item II, the change might have occurred over the course of a million years or more. In the case of item IV, 6,000 years can conceivably include 3,000 generations (Red Deer mature at age 2). Therefore, in both items II and IV, the apparent sudden change could have actually occurred gradually.

95.   **What is convergent evolution?**
       (Average) (Skill 16.3)

      A.   The development of closely related species

      B.   The development of unrelated species that do not share similar biological structures

      C.   The development of similar biological structures in similar species

      D.   The development of similar biological structures in unrelated (or distantly related) species

Answer: D. The development of similar biological structures in unrelated (or distantly related) species

Convergent evolution is the development of similar biological structures in unrelated (or distantly related) species. The traits emerged not because the species share a recent common ancestor, but because the species were adapting to similar environmental factors or situations.

INTERDEPENDENCE AND BEHAVIOR OF ORGANISMS

96.   **What is commensalism?**
       (Easy) (Skill 17.2)

      A.   One predator eating another species as its prey

      B.   One species benefiting from the another without causing any harm to the other species

      C.   Competition for resources such as habitat, food, and mates

      D.   One predator species living on or in another species causing detrimental effects to the host

Answer: B. One species benefiting from the another without causing any harm to the other species

Commensalism occurs when one species benefits from the other without causing any harm to the other species.

97. **The first cells that evolved on earth were probably of which type?**
    (Average) (Skill 18.1)

    A. Autotrophs

    B. Eukaryotes

    C. Heterotrophs

    D. Prokaryotes

Answer: D. Prokaryotes
Prokaryotes were first observed in the fossil record 3.5 billion years ago. Their ability to adapt to the environment allows them to thrive in a wide variety of habitats.

98. **All of the following are density-dependent factors that affect a population except:**
    (Rigorous) (Skill 18.1)

    A. Disease

    B. Drought

    C. Predation

    D. Migration

Answer: B. Drought
Although drought would affect the amount of food available to a population (which creates a density-dependent factor), the drought itself would occur regardless of population size, and is thus density-independent. Disease and migration tend to occur more frequently in crowded populations. The amount of prey and predators would affect the number of individuals in a population.

99. **Which of the following is *not* an example of dynamic equilibrium? (Rigorous) (Skill 18.1)**

    A.   A stable population

    B.   A symbiotic pair of organisms

    C.   Osmoregulation

    D.   Maintaining head position while walking

Answer: D. Maintaining head position while walking
Maintinaing head position while walking is a case of static equilibrium, a state where things do not change. In a stable population, birth and death rates must be the same. In a symbiotic pair, the contributions of each organism must be equivalent, or the relationship becomes parasitic. Osmoregulation balances the body's need for water and the dissolved compounds within it.

100. **All of the following are density-independent factors that affect a population except: (Average) (Skill 18.1)**

    A.   Temperature

    B.   Rainfall

    C.   Predation

    D.   Soil nutrients

Answer: C. Predation
As a population increases, the competition for resources intensifies and the growth rate declines. This is a density-dependent factor. An example of this would be predation. Density-independent factors affect the population regardless of its size. Examples of density-independent factors are rainfall, temperature, and soil nutrients.